EDMUND WILSON

Edmund Wilson

CENTENNIAL
REFLECTIONS

LEWIS M. DABNEY

EDITOR

THE MERCANTILE LIBRARY OF NEW YORK

IN ASSOCIATION WITH

PRINCETON UNIVERSITY PRESS

PRINCETON, NEW JERSEY

Copyright © 1997 by Princeton University Press;
"Edmund Wilson: Three Phases" © 1997 by Morris Dickstein;
"Wilson's Modernism" © 1997 by David Bromwich;
contributions to "Omissions in *Patriotic Gore*" © 1997 by
Randall Kennedy, David Bromwich, and Toni Morrison
Published by Princeton University Press, 41 William Street,
Princeton, New Jersey 08540
In the United Kingdom: Princeton University Press,
Chichester, West Sussex

Library of Congress Cataloging-in-Publication Data
will be found on the last printed page of this book

Quotations from Wilson's writing and from the letters of Elena Wilson
are used by permission of Farrar, Straus, & Giroux and of
Helen Miranda Wilson, executrix of the Estate of Helen Wilson

Publication of this book has been aided by
the Mercantile Library of New York

This book has been composed in Caledonia
Designed by Jan Lilly
Composed by Eileen Reilly

Princeton University Press books are printed on acid-free paper and
meet the guidelines for permanence and durability of the
Committee on Production Guidelines for Book Longevity of the
Council on Library Resources

Printed in the United States of America

1   3   5   7   9   10   8   6   4   2

(Pbk.)

1   3   5   7   9   10   8   6   4   2

CONTENTS

PERSPECTIVES

CONTRIBUTORS

DANIEL AARON, professor emeritus of English and American literature at Harvard University, is currently at work on a historical memoir.

PAUL BERMAN, author of *A Tale of Two Utopias: The Political Journey of the Generation of 1968*, contributes to *Dissent*, the *New Republic*, and the *New Yorker*. His next book includes a full-length essay on Wilson.

DAVID BRADLEY is the author of *South Street* and *The Chaneysville Incident*.

DAVID BROMWICH, professor of English at Yale University, is the author of *Hamlet and the Mind of a Critic*, *A Choice of Inheritance*, and *Politics by Other Means*.

LEWIS M. DABNEY, who teaches English at the University of Wyoming, edited Wilson's *The Sixties: The Last Journal* as well as *The Portable Edmund Wilson* and *The Edmund Wilson Reader*.

ANDREW DELBANCO, Levi Professor in the Humanities at Columbia University, is the author of *The Puritan Ordeal* and *The Death of Satan: How Americans Have Lost the Sense of Evil*. His work appears in the *New York Review of Books*, the *New Republic*, and other journals.

MORRIS DICKSTEIN teaches English at Queens College and the CUNY Graduate School, where he directs the Center for the Humanities. He is author of *Gates of Eden: American Culture in the Sixties* and, most recently, *Double Agent: The Critic and Society*.

BARBARA EPSTEIN coedits the *New York Review of Books*.

JASON EPSTEIN is vice president and editorial director at Random House.

ELIZABETH HARDWICK publishes most of her essays in the *New York Review of Books*, where she is advisory editor. Her next book of criticism will contain an essay on Wilson.

ANN HULBERT, author of *The Interior Castle: The Art and Life of Jean Stafford*, is a contributing editor of the *New Republic* and a freelance writer in Washington.

ALFRED KAZIN's criticism of American literature began with *On Native Grounds* in 1942. His latest book is *A Lifetime Burning in Every Moment*, drawn from his journals.

RANDALL KENNEDY teaches at Harvard Law School and edits *Reconstruction*. He is the author of *Race, Crime, and the Law*.

MARK KRUPNICK teaches in the Divinity School, the Department of English, and the Committee for Jewish Studies at the University of Chicago. He is the author of *Lionel Trilling and the Fate of Cultural Criticism* and of numerous articles and reviews.

MICHAEL C. D. MACDONALD is a journalist and the author of *America's Cities: A Report on the Myth of Urban Renaissance*.

MARY MEIGS's autobiography is *Lily Briscoe: A Self-Portrait*. A painter as well as a memoirist, she appeared in the film *Strangers in Good Company*.

LOUIS MENAND teaches English at the Graduate School of the City University of New York and writes for various journals. He is the author of *Discovering Modernism: T. S. Eliot and His Context* and has most recently edited *A Portable Pragmatism*.

SHELDON MEYER is senior editor at the Oxford University Press.

TONI MORRISON, who won the Nobel Prize for literature in 1993, teaches at Princeton University.

JED PERL is art critic for the *New Republic* and author of *Paris Without End: On French Art Since World War I* and *Gallery Going: Four Seasons in the Art World*.

NEALE REINITZ is professor emeritus of English at Colorado College.

DAVID REMNICK is the author of *Lenin's Tomb* and *Resurrection*.

JAMES A. SANDERS, professor of theology and director of the Ancient Biblical Manuscript Center at Claremont College, is known for his work on the Scroll of Psalms from Qumran Cave Eleven. His forthcoming book is called *The Impact of the Dead Sea Scrolls on Biblical Studies*.

ARTHUR SCHLESINGER, JR., is a historian and writer.

ROGER STRAUS is president of Farrar, Straus & Giroux.

MICHAEL WALZER teaches in the School of Social Science at the Institute for Advanced Study. His books include *The Company of Critics*.

SEAN WILENTZ is director of the Program in American Studies and Professor of History at Princeton University. A contributing editor of the *New Republic*, he also writes for the *New York Times Book Review*, and is the author of *Chants Democratic: New York City and the Rise of the American Working Class, 1788–1850*.

C. VANN WOODWARD is Sterling Professor Emeritus of History at Yale University.

EDMUND WILSON

INTRODUCTION

LEWIS M. DABNEY

MAY 8, 1995, marked the centenary of the birth of
Edmund Wilson—the thinker, writer, critic, and "cultural man-of-all-work" who helped shape American literature for fifty years of the twentieth century and
whose influence reaches us yet. Once the youthful
dean of criticism in the '20s, mentoring and promoting
talents as diverse as F. Scott Fitzgerald and Ernest
Hemingway, then social commentator and radical intellectual spirit of the '30s, and for three decades there-
after selecting books and cultures to explore from his
pulpit at the *New Yorker*, Wilson lives on in print. He
has influenced a coming generation of readers and
thinkers about art and society, and his name is regu-
larly invoked in the book reviews and literary quarter-
lies. His style, which William Shawn, his editor for
many years, believed one of the best in the history of
English prose, continues to exemplify the fusion of
lucidity, force, and ease.

Thus readers, some of whom had followed Wilson
during his lifetime and others who encounter him
only now, honored the critic at a series of Wednesday

evenings in April and May at Manhattan's Mercantile
Library. A second symposium, held at Princeton University on a November weekend, focused on major
themes of his work and the books that carry them.
Speakers at the two occasions ranged from English
professors, journalists, and publishers to historians of
ideas, anthropologists, biblical scholars, and others
whose fields Wilson had illumined. They aired a variety of viewpoints on his role and significance in American letters, and there were impromptu exchanges between the panelists and with the audience. This book
arises from those meetings.

Wilson was himself a colossal reader, devouring libraries and submerging himself in foreign languages
in an attempt to get closer to the authors he studied,
just as he quizzed acquaintances with a journalistic
zeal when fastening on a new subject. He lived up to
his requirement that to evaluate a book one should be
familiar with the entire body of the author's work and
its national and international contexts. He wrote almost
every day, often in more than one form, and published
nearly everything he wrote, then republished it, polished and sometimes expanded, finding ways, as he
once said of Poe, to make editors "pay him for the
gratuitous labor of rewriting demanded by his artistic
conscience." Not since Sainte-Beuve, whose weekly
literary articles spanned thirty years of the mid–nineteenth century, or Saintsbury, the connoisseur of English and French literature at the century's end, has
another matched that range of production and discrimi-
nation. And Wilson is a much better critic than Sainte-
Beuve or Saintsbury. His blending of biography and

character studies with literary analysis makes him the successor of Johnson as well as Taine in the arena of literary portraiture.

A literary journalism so energetic and so well-informed as this could function as a counterweight to the academy. Not imposing the stamp of a codified system upon each individual act of interpretation, Wilson carried within himself the ability to digest an idea, stance, or book before him, an individual writer or entire movement, through an ever-expanding knowledge of culture and history animated by intuition and emotion. The discerning enthusiasm of the young critic who believed that Joyce, Proust, and Yeats were accessible to the man in the street could later vivify the Zuñi pueblo and imagine the lost sect that had produced the Dead Sea Scrolls. Judgment was part of his job, he knew, but judgment was subjective, and he had also to convey the living spirit of what he read and saw, enabling readers to make their own evaluations. Sifting literature through personality and milieu, in the tradition of nineteenth-century historicism, Wilson absorbed Freud and Marx without being tempted to define a book through its origins in the unconscious or an ideological subtext. He was not without intellectual rigor, albeit attentive to the individual human voice when searching for truth in revolutionary movements. He ventured into the realm of unanswerable questions, such as the connection between art and personal ordeal, for which there is no empirical test or adequate general formula. If he did not resolve such riddles for his readers, at least one always had the assurance that the tour guide knew the terrain through which he had successfully guided one. And if Wilson was not a specialist in many of the areas he explored, his broad brush achieved a fine precision.

While the New Critics, teaching readers how to absorb a text's complexities, thought Wilson too much the popularizer, he effectively challenged their abstraction of literature from its human scene. Their successors in academe, applying the theories of European thinkers, have lacked opponents with his authority in the larger literary world. Until recently, they have seemed too narrowly dedicated to philosophical and social programs to pay much attention to someone whose best work is involved with innumerable particular interests, and for whom intellectual inquiry is no more urgent a cause than writing itself—witness Wilson's fiction, poetry, plays, and journals. New adherents, though, have come to his side, caught by his excitement over a work or subject and luxuriating in the sweeping vistas he opens up, never patronizing nor pretentious, but rather like the fresh-voiced narrator of a realistic novel who opens up new insights and experiences. He stands beside the great modern novelists and poets who have defined our twentieth-century literature. A recent issue of the *New Yorker* reprints a brilliant letter from Pasternak responding to Wilson's account of the symbolism in *Doctor Zhivago*; not long afterward, in the *New York Times*, a reviewer of a theatrical performance of *The Waste Land* cites Wilson on the poem's dramatic character.

His value as an interpreter of literature and culture today is complemented rather than obscured by his versatility as a man of letters. Periodically published, beginning with *A Prelude* and *The Twenties*, which he himself edited, the journals have kept before readers Wilson's life and his vision of the times. These six volumes, with his widow Elena's collection of his letters, are a source for historical scholars and others writing about Wilson's contemporaries, from Scott Fitzgerald to Nabokov and Dawn Powell. The series was completed in 1993 with the publication of *The Sixties*. The centenary year brought Jeffrey Meyers's biography, as well as Janet Groth and David Castronovo's *From the Uncollected Edmund Wilson*, a gathering of reviews and other short pieces largely of his youth. On his birthday in May, Wilson was the subject of an hour on National Public Radio. His unpublished novella of the '20s (to be called *The Higher Jazz*) is being edited by Neale Reinitz for the University of Iowa Press, and Da Capo is bringing out *The Edmund Wilson Reader*, an expanded version of the Viking *Portable.*

The future course of literary studies will determine Wilson's place in the tradition. Will he survive as, say, Johnson and Boswell survive? Attention will be paid to his unflagging patriotism, a loyalty to the American Republic matching that to the republic of letters, as well as the pragmatism and work ethic that, with the bulk of his output and the industry invested in the task, link him more closely to the Victorians than to the modern spirit with which he identified. If he grew pessimistic at the end, he persisted in the rationalist's conviction that the labor of the mind could help to move humanity ahead. "The only thing that we can make is our work," reads his well-known letter to Louise Bogan. "And deliberate work of the mind, imagination, and hand, done, as Nietzsche said, 'not-withstanding,' in the long run remakes the world." We cannot easily extract Wilson's literary idealism and his individualism from their scene, drawing upon his strengths for our own purposes. But we can call attention to his enduring insights and the values which he captured on the page, even as we put together the complex story of his life and work, which incorporates so much of the cultural life of twentieth-century America. We can aim for the same completeness of vision he had upon his subjects.

This volume continues the current of thought about Wilson by carrying into print voices from the two symposiums. Neither paean nor assessment, the book interweaves the perspectives of a number of distin-guished figures from the fields he worked in, who, in coming together to discuss his writing, also consider lit-erary tradition, social events and consequences, and criticism as an art. The first section establishes Wilson's premises. Morris Dickstein's essay traces the evolution of a young man with Keatsian receptivity into the for-midably solid figure of the '50s and '60s. Jason Epstein then takes Wilson as an apostle of reason convinced that human beings could reshape their world if they but had the will, while Barbara Epstein stresses his ro-mantic temperament. Though Wilson came to dislike the classification, David Bromwich subtly understands the way in which he was a modernist, correlating his assumptions with his style. Jed Perl investigates Wilson's responses, over half a century, to art and music, capturing the precision with which he trans-posed images to the page. Turning to a central theme of the later work, Mark Krupnick elucidates the bearing of a Protestant-Puritan heritage on Wilson's interest in Jews and Judaism.

Neale Reinitz's essay on the journals and their composition opens the next part, directing us toward the personality behind the writing. My biographical chapter explores a critical moment in Wilson's life, at the turning point that preceded his major books. What his example and his teaching meant in the literary world after World War II can be seen in the informal reminiscences of Elizabeth Hardwick, Jason Epstein, Mary Meigs, Roger Straus, and Alfred Kazin. Michael Macdonald provides a view of the critic's domestic scene at the Cape, through the eyes of an awestruck young family friend. James Sanders, whom Wilson consulted about the Dead Sea Scrolls, reconsiders Wilson's account of them, noticing sound judgments which, Sanders says, as a brash young scholar he had taken less seriously.

The third part features *To the Finland Station* and *Patriotic Gore*. After David Remnick looks, through the lens of contemporary developments, at Wilson's reaction to the Soviet Union in 1935 and the book completed five years later, Daniel Aaron clarifies the nature of his upper-class socialist idealism. There follows an exchange which grew to involve other speakers as well as the audience, meriting its inclusion here. The second subject, Wilson's book about the literature of the Civil War era, is introduced by a debate about how far the oft-discussed polemical preface accords with *Patriotic Gore*'s individual portraits. Randall Kennedy's own polemic on the subject of Wilson's alleged indifference to black America—though not to Haitian blacks who wrote in French—is here somewhat shortened, and coupled to reactions from panel and audience members. David Bradley laments that the background of segregation kept the explorer of exotic minority communities from looking into his own backyard. Finally, Andrew Delbanco traces *Patriotic Gore*'s roots in the Americanized Protestantism that sustained the critic after the failure of his radical ideals, noting how a writer can derive sustenance from a spiritual heritage even as he mourns its corruption into dogmatism and violence.

In the last part of this book, Louis Menand and Paul Berman offer divergent but complementary approaches to the subject of Wilson in his historical moment and in ours, each stressing his change of direction in the 1940s. Menand reminds intellectual conservatives how far removed Wilson was from the values of Middle America as well as the cause of the great books of the West. And though his frame of reference was in some sense canonical—the Greeks and Dante, Flaubert and Tolstoy, were as important to him as Proust and Joyce—he reached out to other cultures and relished discovering writers outside the mainstream. Berman sees Wilson's example liberating scholars and journalists of his own generation from sterile academic theory. This doesn't solve the problem of those graduate students who, for many years now, have expected, as a dissident theorist says, to be "chastised" when they "refuse analytical terminologies" for the sake of "writing criticism in the experiential, nonprofessional mode, the mode of Pater, Woolf, Hazlitt,

Ruskin, and in fact of Edmund Wilson." Wilson's voice, in any event, was unique, and it seems unlikely that there will be either an academic or journalistic critic to succeed him.

What makes him a useful model is that he sides with both the intellectual struggling to make sense of life and the writer immersing himself in what Conrad called its "destructive element." Each is for Wilson an outsider, receiving what support he can from the past, remote from the trendy success stories of our culture. His stance is dramatized in the early mono- logue "A Preface to Persius," where an eighteenth-cen- tury Englishman's sympathetic commentary on a rough-hewn Roman satirist moves Wilson to sum up the task of civilization and "the paradox of literature": born of a painful, even chaotic reality with which it must stay in touch, it derives from our need "to strike some permanent mark of the mind on the mysterious flux of experience which escapes beneath our hand." This and other Wilsonian credos were passed over in our centenary conversation's emphasis on the great biographical chronicles *Finland Station* and *Patriotic Gore*. Converging upon the role of the individual in history and the validity of progressive ideals, those books made a natural focus. Of necessity, however, much was left out or foreshortened, including *The Triple Thinkers*, *The Wound and the Bow*, and later lit- erary portraiture, where Wilson is on solid ground. The theme of his intellectual life is not the dominance of politics—as in America today, when critics often speak for social groups and always keep their sensibilities in mind—but the endurance and triumph of literature.

Robert Lowell noted Wilson's quiet confidence at a White House dinner given by John Kennedy. When the president, with his own interest in literature and history, asked what *Patriotic Gore* had taught him about the meaning of the Civil War, Wilson simply suggested that he read the book.

The choice and order of the material here are mine. I regret the loss of certain moments and speakers that could not be integrated into the format of the volume— Denis Donoghue's observation that although Wilson was not really a student of language, his own language will be closely studied; Wendy Lesser's belief that Wilson had a better eye than he did an ear, yet could hear the music of great poetry. A number of talks from the symposiums have been expanded by their authors. Everything has been edited, including the discussions, without, it is hoped, sacrificing their spontaneity. I am indebted to Garry Alkire for a range of vital editorial help; to Harold Augenbraum, Director of the Mercantile Library, and Robert Disch of Hunter College, who helped organize the evenings in New York, and to John Young of the Florence Gould Foundation for support of the whole project; as well as to Sean Wilentz and Princeton University Press. It was Wilentz who, at the Princeton conference, put together a younger generation of journalists and scholars whose energy, in this book, combines with the understanding of those acquainted with Wilson's times and, in greater or less degree, the man. Wilentz, appropriately, has the final word.

THE CRITIC AND

HIS PREMISES

EDMUND WILSON:

THREE PHASES

MORRIS DICKSTEIN

A CENTENNIAL celebration provides the occasion to take a fresh look at a writer's work, to pay tribute and examine the legacy. We can profit from this when the writing still somehow lives, still has meaning for a new generation. In the case of a critic this is unusual because criticism, unlike literature, is cumulative, developing from one generation to another as critics build on their predecessors by exploding or assimilating them. Unless it survives on style alone, criticism, as mediation between writers and readers, quickly grows dated, and critics are more likely to be forgotten than reconsidered. Wilson's criticism, however, is an exception—we can go back to his early readings of Hemingway or Fitzgerald in the 1920s and still respond strongly to them.

In the past few years we've learned a great deal about Wilson the man. We've had seven volumes of diaries, a large and very readable selection of letters, a separate edition of his correspondence with Vladimir

Nabokov, a number of biographies and memoirs by and about Mary McCarthy in which Wilson figures more or less as the villain, and most recently, a widely reviewed biography by Jeffrey Meyers. While respectful of Wilson the writer and trying hard to imagine the marriage to McCarthy from Wilson's point of view, Meyers's biography focuses too much on the almost clinical lover, the difficult husband, the distracted, intermittent father, the imperious personality. What we need, among other things, is a scrupulous and detailed intellectual biography, which Meyers's book does not pretend to be. While it's of a certain interest, if it's true, to be told that Wilson and his friend John Peale Bishop "made simultaneous love to" Edna St. Vincent Millay—I forget which one took the upper half and which took the lower—I don't see how it adds anything to our sense of Wilson as a writer. There should be a way at his hundredth birthday to go back to his work, to ask essential questions about whether he still engages us as contemporary readers, and about his precise connections to the cultural and political life of his own times.

He was a commanding figure between the 1920s and the early 1970s, and only H. L. Mencken has been as posthumously prolific. I'm struck by the extraordinary variety in his huge body of writing, from the drama and fiction and poetry, at which he was not very successful, to the travel writing that supports much of his later work. One can think of his career as an itinerary, as he himself once tried to do in notes for an autobiographical novel. His early criticism, however, is an extraordinary point of departure. Besides introducing his reading public to American writers and the difficult modernists—about some of whom he wrote some of the first articles to appear in the American press—he also wrote about Chaplin movies, popular culture, vaudeville, and the Ziegfeld Follies. Nothing better illuminates the conditions under which Wilson worked than the essays collected in *The Shores of Light*, which recall the glory days of Wilson as a critic, a man wonderfully in tune with the new literary movements. In its profusion and abundance, it is both the best collection of his journalism and a fascinating literary chronicle of the era. The excitement of discovery fills the ninety-seven articles, only a selection of what he published during that period. Today, we no longer have a critic writing weekly essays for a magazine like the *New Republic*, his main forum during the '20s and '30s. His old nemesis, Stanley Edgar Hyman, who once dismissed Wilson as a mere journalist, was the last to try it in the *New Leader* in the 1960s. Perhaps the collected literary journalism of John Updike and Gore Vidal comes closest to Wilson's in scope, though without his daunting critical authority. His was a nineteenth-century approach to criticism, the generalist as man of letters— judicial, didactic, authoritative—within a much more book-oriented culture.

In one anonymously published twenty-page piece called "The All-Star Literary Vaudeville," he offered a sweeping yet entertaining account of nearly every writer on the contemporary scene. Like an expert tour guide, he takes on these writers, with a no-nonsense directness that would become his hallmark and a remarkable self-assurance about what he thinks of each

one. These really are encounters, a favorite word of his
during the period. And even when he is wrongheaded
or rudimentary, he engages the writers, some of them
new and difficult, with the full weight of his own experience and sensibility. If a case can be made against
the Wilson of *The Shores of Light*, it is that his almost
perfect pitch for prose fiction deserts him when he
turns to poetry. He favors friends like Elinor Wylie or
Millay, while doing scant justice to major figures like
Robert Frost, Wallace Stevens, Hart Crane, or William
Carlos Williams. Not really a technical critic, he excels
at connecting writers to their milieu, an approach more
suited to the social and biographical texture of fiction
than to the linguistic density of poetry.

What makes the pieces so impressive when you reread them is not only his range but the agility and flexibility of his dealings with different kinds of writers. In
the middle of the book he slips in a manifesto called
"The Critic Who Does Not Exist" in which he maps out
the warring critical and literary schools of the time,
each propagating its own doctrine while paying no
attention to other viewpoints, and with no genuinely
disinterested critic ("that is, a writer who is at once
first-rate and nothing but a literary critic") prepared to
challenge them with hard questions. Wilson clearly
saw himself as just that critic, someone who could
move easily among many kinds of writers, not con-
strained by dogma or party spirit, committed omnivo-
rously to literature itself in all its protean variety. He
once confessed that he loved to talk about writers to
people who hadn't yet encountered them—the opposite of an academic critic who writes for the already

initiated. This love of introducing a writer to an audience enabled Wilson to give free play to the narrative gifts never fully realized in his fiction. When he writes about Proust and Joyce in *Axel's Castle*, he actually sets about to re-create these writers—not simply to rehearse the story but to convey it in a way so nuanced with criticism, interpretation, irony, and judgment that it unfolds as a whole new thing, a redaction that is itself novelistic.

Assembling these articles in 1952, long after they first appeared, Wilson dramatized his critical position with a witty juxtaposition, setting a piece on H. L. Mencken alongside one on Woodrow Wilson's tenure as president of Princeton. We would normally think of Mencken and Woodrow Wilson as polar opposites— Wilson so moralistic, impassioned, rhetorical; Mencken ever the iconoclast, eagerly deflating moralistic cant. But the young critic presents them to us as two rigidly determined minds, repetitious and predictably themselves. A part of Wilson is drawn to this: it helps explain his lifelong interest in the effects of New England Puritanism on later American culture. At the end of each piece he makes a dialectical turn, showing how Mencken's dogmatism gives him power as a satirist and honoring Woodrow Wilson's equally inflexible idealism, which would cause him so much trouble in his conflict with the U.S. Senate. The young man sympathizes with both positions, especially with the sort of idealism that was in short supply during the Coolidge years, when he wrote his piece. Yet the critical temperament, as he understood it, was the reverse of what these men possessed, for they were strongly defined personalities who always knew exactly who and what they were. The later Edmund Wilson would become quite magisterial, but in the '20s he found in himself the Keatsian negative capability that opened up to an enormous range of literary experiences. And the innovative, devil-may-care spirit of the decade was exactly the setting for such a critic.

The 1920s concluded for him with the publication of *Axel's Castle* in 1931, and this established a pattern for subsequent stages of his career. If the reviews collected in *The Shores of Light* show Wilson as the working critic, the writer in the trenches meeting each new book as it comes, *Axel's Castle* is the summation that rounds off the period, the larger synthesis with which he took leave of each phase of his literary life. He reached for permanence in the same way with *To the Finland Station* (1940), which provided a coda for his Marxist adventure of the 1930s, and *Patriotic Gore* (1962), the enduring result of his return, in the 1940s and '50s, to American culture and his own origins.

It's characteristic of these longer, more ambitious projects that Wilson, conscientious puritan that he was, persisted and carried through with them long after he had outlived the original impulse to write them. He had already converted to socialism by the time he completed his study of the modernists, just as he'd grown disaffected with Marxism and the Soviet Union when he put the finishing touches on his extended account of the revolutionary tradition up through 1917. This is a tribute to Wilson's work ethic—he'd started and was damn well going to finish—but it gives these books a slightly odd character, even a certain incoherence. In *Axel's Castle*, for example, the great chapters on Proust and Joyce portray them not simply as formal innovators but as social observers deeply involved with the life of their times. But by the end of the book he comes close to condemning them for retreating to a symbolist castle, an impenetrable fastness of art for art's sake—precisely what he had already shown they did *not* do.

Wilson's shifting views create a fissure within the book. They also led to his political activism of those years: the 1931 manifesto in which he urged liberals, radicals, and progressives to "take Communism away from the Communists"; the Depression journalism and travel writing collected in *The American Jitters* and *Travels in Two Democracies*; and, finally, his account of the socialist spirit as it culminated in the Russian Revolution, *To the Finland Station*. This book resulted from his conversion to radicalism, which had led him to take to the road for the *New Republic* to cover the human effects of the Depression, doing real reporting, not simply literary journalism. Wilson would insist that the Depression had hit America with the impact of a flood or an earthquake, a vast cataclysm that altered the whole landscape. Like many young intellectuals, he had already been skeptical of the booming business civilization of the 1920s; for them, as he later said in "The Literary Consequences of the Crash," written for *The Shores of Light*, "these years were not depressing but stimulating. One couldn't help being exhilarated at the sudden unexpected collapse of that stupid gigantic fraud. It gave us a new sense of freedom."

While setting out to report on how ordinary Americans were coping with the hard times, he gradually conceived the project of writing a biographical history of the entire revolutionary tradition—an unlikely enterprise for someone with little economic or political background. *To the Finland Station* holds up today, I think, as his greatest book—not so much as intellectual history—was never seriously engaged with the intricacies of Marxist dialectics—but as sheer human drama, an immense sweep that can still carry us along even in these postutopian times. Putting aside the sectarian polemics and scholastic debates so often fatal to radical intellectuals, he was able to bring something unique to bear upon Marxism—the same critical sensibility he had brought to modernism. He examined Saint-Simon and Marx with all the curiosity he had just focused on T. S. Eliot and Gertrude Stein.

Many years later, V. S. Pritchett described *To the Finland Station* as "perhaps the only book on the grand scale to come out of the Thirties—in either England or America. It contains, to a novel degree, the human history of an argument." *To a novel degree*: this is a finely phrased remark. It's ironic, in the light of Wilson's limitations as a novelist, that *To the Finland Station* has many of the qualities of great fiction—a bold narrative thrust, striking, larger-than-life characters—combined with Wilson's mixture of irony and empathy toward these outsized, eccentric figures. In a review in *Partisan Review* in 1940, Meyer Schapiro described how Wilson's portraits "impose themselves by their concreteness, finesse, and sympathy . . . like the great fictional characters of literature." But he also showed the connection to the author himself by noting that in this book "the conditions of intellectual work become as concrete, as unforgettable, as the moments of action." Wilson's figures from the Marxist tradition are, above all, intellectuals, men caught up, as he was, with a passion for altering and affecting history. Wilson put flesh and blood on the revolutionary tradition.

Denis Donoghue has described a literary critic as one who puts pressure on a writer's language, but there are different ways to focus on language, as there are different kinds of critics. Always the portraitist, the historian of motive and behavior, in books like *To the Finland Station* and *Patriotic Gore* Wilson bears down on language as a key to individual temperament. He looks closely at Marx's writings, including his early poetry and work as a student, exploring the imagery to grasp the configurations of the writer's mind. This was quite dramatic in the 1930s, when Marxism was invariably debated as doctrine and ideology, not as the written traces of an individual mind. Later he would examine General Grant's letters and memoirs similarly, for he was interested not only in style but in language as the basis for a social or psychological portrait, very much like developing a character in fiction. Wilson begins his third major project, *Patriotic Gore*, with an unlikely revolutionary, Harriet Beecher Stowe, whose extraordinarily *humane* exposure of the Southern slave system derives from her faith in family values and her reading of the character of its participants. But the book finds its center in the unflappable figure of Grant—a man utterly unconscious of danger in battle who, in the teeth of great suffering as a dying man, finished his memoirs in order to provide for his family after his death. "In what Grant did and in what he wrote," Wilson finds "the driving force, the exalted moral certainty, of Lincoln and Mrs. Stowe." He admires not only Grant the man but also the plain stylist, capable of expressing exactly what he wanted to say with strength and simplicity, "in the fewest well-chosen words." Grant's writing, with its "literary qualities," says Wilson, provides "evidence of a natural fineness of character, mind, and taste."

The book emerged from Wilson's intense dissatisfaction with contemporary America after 1940—which also led to his withdrawal to upstate New York, his turn to autobiography, his fascination with his own family background, and his gradual disengagement from the contemporary critical scene. *Patriotic Gore* demonstrates not only his recoil into the American past but his attraction to those qualities—essentially qualities of republican virtue—that he could not find in the public world of the American present. If *To the Finland Station* is about personality, as expressed in a fierce, youthful passion to change the world, *Patriotic Gore* focuses on character, as reflected in traits like stoicism, persistence, fortitude, skepticism, and clarity of mind. Wilson's new heroes are no longer intellectuals but aging warriors like Grant, Lee, Sherman, and that staunch ex-warrior, Justice Oliver Wendell Holmes.

So this, I think, is where Wilson himself came to rest, as an old man perhaps identifying himself with Grant's infirmities as well as his temperament, admiring "the dynamic force and definiteness of his personality"—Wilson as a rock-ribbed American character, no longer the Keatsian seismograph of the cultural and political scene around him but withdrawn, like his father before him, into "a pocket of the past." He could be immensely eloquent about this "old fogeyism," as he liked to describe it, at one point calling himself a man more or less of the eighteenth century, at other times a man of the twenties. But for all of the diversity of his interests in his last years—exploring Russian literature, learning Hebrew and writing about the Dead Sea Scrolls, going to Haiti, studying Hungarian—in the end he became something of a nativist whose fundamental values were invested in a Roman and republican ideal he linked to people like Grant and Holmes. In the peroration to *Patriotic Gore*, after eight hundred pages, he describes the aged Holmes as "perhaps the last Roman" as "a just man, a man of the old America, who having proved himself early in the Civil War, had persisted and continued to function through everything that had happened since, and had triumphed in remaining faithful to some kind of traditional ideal."

What an odd yet moving place for Edmund Wilson's last phase: the free-living modernist of the 1920s transformed into the quintessential American of an earlier era, the receptive critic into the eccentric, quirky Johnsonian figure we knew from Wilson's later years. It may well be that the more we learn about Wilson's personal life the less we like him. But he lived his writing life on a heroic scale. Wilson can be compared to the great Victorians in his plenitude and persistence, in the strength of his work ethic and the sense of moral calling he brought to the practice of criticism. His curiosity and gift for languages kept him from turning provincial. At a time when other critics grew enamored of technique, he used everything from social history and biography to psychoanalysis to hold fast to the elusive human dimension of literature. He saw reading and writing as personal encounters, the fruits of each person's unique sensibility, and he never lost confidence in his own power to make sense of his impressions, to translate other people's language into limpid, terse, and resonant language of his own. As his personal presence fades, the real Edmund Wilson, the one who matters most, survives in his books.

THE RELIGION OF THE ENLIGHTENMENT

JASON EPSTEIN

BY THE TIME Wilson was ten years old the fundamental laws of nature, that is, the laws governing all the parts of the universe including our physical selves, were found to be quite different from what had been understood thus far, and far more humbling even than Galileo's discovery of our fragility and remoteness had been. The discovery of X-rays, radioactivity, the substructure of the atom, relativity, quantum physics, the uncertainty principle, which Heisenberg would announce before Wilson turned thirty, required a new and untranslatable language, one which, for all his linguistic curiosity, he would never learn. One might say this new language was truly the fundamental language of his age, as well as of the universe, which should be understandable by whatever other articulate creatures might share with us the vastness of space. These physical discoveries would produce an epochal transformation within the critic's lifetime. When he died twenty-odd years ago, it was possible to foresee an even greater and more disturbing transformation, for by then the likelihood, perhaps the inevitability, that human beings could soon intervene in the process of our own natural selection was clear, while we ourselves were nowhere near the ethical consensus required to survive such knowledge.

By the time Wilson was twelve, Picasso had painted *Les Demoiselles d'Avignon*; a year later Schoenberg abandoned tonality; four years later, when Wilson was a student at Princeton, the *Titanic* went down, along with the complacency of the age. By the time he graduated, the Great War had introduced a degree of political uncertainty, not to say absurdity, into everyday life, which subsequent events would only amplify. He was in *Axel's Castle* and elsewhere the first and best reporter from the margins where these changes were taking place.

In his later years it was possible for Wilson to wonder, as he did in more than one conversation with me, whether our species could control, for the sake of its survival, the consequence of its ingenuity. Was there something lacking in the human design, he once asked me, some failure of generosity and wisdom that made our survival problematic and our presence on earth a possible disaster? To understand the depth of Wilson's concern about the transgression of the laws of nature as he perhaps naively understood them, we should recall his profound, one might even say zany, conservatism on these matters, his opposition, for example, to vaccination as interference with natural selection, and his rejection of Elena's attempt to exterminate the rats that had invaded his Wellfleet house. Wilson felt strongly that nature should be observed, not interfered with at the expense of its other inhabitants, including even the smallpox bacillus, to say nothing of the Iroquois, whom he admired. As he grew older, he increasingly worried about this interference with the essential order of things. His confidence in the human prospect trembled most visibly in his notorious introduction to *Patriotic Gore* in 1962. But as far as I know it never gave way to despair. Instead, he found his subject in the cultural and literary consequences of these great shifts, this earthquake, as he once described it—beginning of course with the news he brought to his countrymen of so-called symbolism. By the time he was introducing *Patriotic Gore*, his misgivings about his fellow creatures were in the open. This is why he chose to live in what he called "a pocket of the past," and why toward the end he more often retreated to his ancestral home in a remote valley of upstate New York, where he contemplated with great intensity, as if his equanimity depended on it, the residual wisdom to be found in the tribal past: the Iroquois past, the American past, the Hebrew past.

What especially fascinated him about these tribes, including his own, was how they had given continuing authority to their moral values by creating a god or gods or their equivalent who commanded these values, how these tribes had invented and placed beyond human reach the caretakers of their own standards, so that even in the worst of times there would be something to hold onto. In this sense, in the years when I knew him he did not live in the wreckage of his own time but had chosen to become, as he put it, "a back number," a living reminder, as I found him wonderfully to be, of an age whose confidence in the power of mind could no longer be so easily justified. Wilson was to the end of his life an unreconstructed if increasingly discouraged man of the Enlightenment, a man of the nineteenth century with his intellectual and moral roots in the eighteenth, who continued to believe, with Vico, that the social world should be the work of men, or, in American terms, that governments derive their just powers from the consent of the governed, with the implied corollary that human societies are on the whole equal to this responsibility, no matter what the evidence to the contrary.

The strength of this conviction may explain why he was able to publish without embarrassment, in the year of the Hitler-Stalin pact, his heroic celebration of Vico's idea although the book looks to Leninism, behind which was its monstrous Stalinist offspring. It did not matter to him that the great enterprise undertaken by the followers of Vico and Michelet turned out in this case disastrously. For Wilson, the adventure of reason, despite its temporary failures, had a fateful quality, and like a religious devotee he was unwilling to believe the worst, no mattter how strong the temptation. The failure of socialism in the Soviet Union did not presuppose the failure of enlightened humanity itself. At the end of *To the Finland Station*, this simply means that we must try again. I do not suggest that Wilson was essentially a social visionary, for he was anything but, yet where the supremacy of reason was concerned, he was incapable of irony. Though we humans may descend to the condition of slugs devouring other slugs, we are also capable of transcendence.

The Enlightenment idea was a religion he never abandoned, no matter how he may have questioned it. Unreason was a subject for reason to contemplate, not the inevitable outcome of human affairs. As for the religions of others, he was of course deeply skeptical—hence his response to the conversion to Roman Catholicism of his friend Allen Tate. His own youthful flirtation with the two great quackeries of his time, the dogmas of Marx and Freud, was brief, yet his interest in these phenomena as literary material persisted. What saved him from dogma was what his friend Auden called dilettantism, his rampant curiosity and the intensity with which he pursued its objects one after another and often several simultaneously, and his possession of a mind so fine that no idea could violate it, at least not for long—to adapt what Eliot said of Henry James. Except of course for the idea he never abandoned, that the monuments of human culture were evidence of the nobility of the species. Wilson's introduction to *Patriotic Gore* was much condemned for its analogy of human behavior to that of sea slugs devouring their kind blindly and stupidly. But to condemn this introduction misses the point, for the chapters that follow show that in the increasing slaughter and stupidity of the war the possibility of transcendence remains: in Holmes and Mrs. Chestnut, in Grant, even in Sherman, and above all of course in Lincoln. We have been and must be yet again more than simply competing slugs.

Consider this passage from an essay Wilson wrote in the '30s, called "The Jumping-Off Place":

The Americans still tend to move westward, and many drift southward toward the sun. San Diego is situated in the extreme southwestern corner of the United States; and since our real westward expansion has come to a standstill, it has become a kind of jumping off-place. On the West coast today the suicide rate is twice that of the Middle-Atlantic coast, and the suicide rate of San Diego has become since 1911 the highest in the United States. . . . Since the depression, the rate has increased. In 1926 there were fifty-seven suicides in San Diego, during 9 months of 1930 there were seventy-one, and between the beginning of January and the end of July '31 there were already thirty-six. Three of these latter are set down in the coroner's record as due to "no work or money"; two to "no work"; one to "ill-health, family troubles and no work"; two to "despondency over financial worries";, one to "financial worry and illness"; one to "health and failure to collect" rent and one due to "rent due him from tenants." . . . These coroners' records in San Diego are melancholy reading indeed. You seem to see the last futile effervescense of the burst of the American adventure. Here our people, so long told to go west to escape from ill-health and poverty, maladjustment and industrial oppression, are discovering that, having come West, their problems and diseases remain and that the ocean bars further flight. Among the sand-colored hotels and power plants, the naval outfitters and waterside cafés, the old spread-roof California houses with their fine grain of gray or yellow clapboards—they come to the end of their resources in the empty California sun. In San Diego, brokers and bankers, architects and citrus ranchers, farmers, housewives, building contractors, salesmen of groceries and real estate, proprietors of pool rooms and music stores, marines and supply-corps lieutenants, machinists, auto mechanics, oil-well drillers, molders, tailors, carpenters, cooks and barbers, soft-drink merchants, teamsters, stage-drivers, longshoremen, laborers—mostly Anglo-saxon whites, though with a certain number of Danes, Swedes, and Germans, and a sprinkling of Chinese, Japanese, Mexicans, Negroes, Indians, and Filipinos—ill, retired, or down their luck, they stuff up the cracks of their doors and quietly turn on the gas; they go into their back sheds or back kitchens and eat ant paste or swallow lysol; they drive their cars into dark alleys, get into the back seat and shoot themselves, they hang themselves in hotel bedrooms, take overdoses of sulphonal or barbital, they slip off to the municipal golf-links and there stab themselves with carving knives; or they throw themselves into the bay, blue and placid where gray battle ships and cruisers guard the limits of their broad-belting nation—already reaching out in the eighties for the sugar plantations of Honolulu.

This is sort of Walt Whitman upside down, but for me it is very much a poem and a wonderful example of how Wilson wrote, and I think an instance of Wilson's

intellectual struggle against the collapse of morale he
here describes.

By the time he wrote his preface to *Patriotic Gore*,
the gulf had widened considerably between the present world and the world of the past, into which he increasingly retreated and where he found the strength
to go on. Once in Talcottville I tried to interest him in
Thomas Mann, whom he had never read, or so he em-
phatically claimed. Mann's characters, I told him, embodied the major ideas of our time, and taken together
these novels formed a kind of Platonic dialogue of the
moment. Impatiently he replied in his high-pitched
voice that he had no interest in abstract ideas, and that
was the end of that.

But in this he was mistaken, for no matter how
strong his doubts, he believed in the power of reason to
grasp and manage a physical and cultural world that
was itself constructed so as to be rationally understood.
In this conviction he was thoroughly American, for the
America to which he'd retreated was after all a quintessential product of the Enlightenment, its one un-
doubted success and proof of its fundamental rightness.
No wonder that he and his friend Nabokov quarreled
so that eventually they barely found a common language, for the ideas that created Wilson's world had
in another manifestation destroyed Nabokov's. That
Wilson's America might also fail did not deter him, and
he died with his faith intact. It was this commitment to
the only religion worthy of his powers that made him a
hero of his time—and, as these centenary symposiums
suggest, of our time as well.

WILSON'S

ROMANTICISM

BARBARA EPSTEIN

WHEN Edmund Wilson slyly introduced himself, in his unsigned 1926 survey "The All-Star Literary Vaudeville," as "a journalist whose professional activities have been chiefly concerned" with what he calls "the American literary movement of the last fifteen years," the description was characteristic in its modesty, its candor, and its teasing edge. These were qualities that made up much of the disguise of a heavily veiled man. This was his "act," the same act that got him into so much trouble with Nabokov, for whom his corrective impulse too often overcame his admiration. There was always something of a game in that famous quarrel, at least on Wilson's side, though the play doubtless got out of hand.

But the directness, the mistrust of the grandiose, the irony do not at all hide the confidence and ease that were also astonishingly evident in Wilson as early as his teens. One sometimes has the impression, reading his early writings, that he had been born in that brown three-piece suit. It seems remarkable that he was only nineteen years old when he wrote: "Although Mr. James insists on the obvious or sometimes on analyzing the trivial at great length, he manages to give as few other novelists do the impression of real human relations with their complexities of motive and cross motive." Remarkable too that only a few months later, then an undergraduate at Princeton, reading *The Brothers Karamazov* for the first time, he remarks to his friend Alfred Bellinger that most writers on Dostoyevsky missed his irony. He himself, he said, saw the novel as "a satire on the Russian people," and he announced his intention to "investigate him further," as we know he did. He was getting at the heart of a writer even then.

As a reporter for the *New Republic* during the '20s and '30s, he covered coal strikes, election campaigns, the Follies, a performance of *Petrushka*. It seems clear that the dailiness of journalism greatly helped him to master the art of plain description and swift impression. In the account of the Coronado Beach Hotel in San Diego, that precedes the catalogue of suicides in "The Jumping-Off Place," one sees how adroitly he can move from meticulous detail and observation to explode into an idea. The hotel in Wilson's article is "the ultimate triumph of the dreams of the architects of the Eighties," and one reads almost breathlessly as its details accumulate—its "five tiers of white-railinged porches like decks," its "exotic palms" and "little red ventilators spinning in the sun"—until the piece takes

its sudden romantic dive, and he observes how his
countrymen "come to the end of their resources in the
empty California sun."

There was something romantic about Wilson's writing, particularly his writing about America—perhaps
because America was the subject of so many of the
pieces he wrote while he was relatively young. But one
finds it even later in so strange and dark a work as *Patriotic Gore*, with its almost passionate admiration of
Ulysses Grant, or in his fascinated attraction to Mrs.
Chestnut, his disappointment in Lincoln. In fact, the
excitement and curiosity Wilson brought to works of
literature throughout his life, the high expectation he
had for writers he admired, and his love affairs with
languages, are products of a deeply romantic temperament. One remembers how he had set out to learn
Hungarian "with a slightly uneasy memory of the senile
Baron Hulot in Balzac tottering up to the attic to em-
bark on his last liaison." Being a romantic, he was
highly susceptible to disappointment. I think this helps
to account for some of the despair he felt in later life.
Yet he never lost that eager anticipation. There's something of it in his letter to Gilbert Highet written only a
few years before Wilson died, when he wonders
whether Highet "happens to know about a new manuscript copy of Petronius that is supposed to have turned
up in Egypt."

Wilson's romantic investments in a writer or a country could, I suppose, lead him astray. It's true that he
became so involved in the literature and life of Haiti
after his trip there in 1949 he was moved to predict that

the next flowering of French poetry was bound to take place in the Caribbean. Could he have seen something that others had not? *The Dead Sea Scrolls*, one of the grandest of his journalistic scoops, is surely a romantic novel, with lonely heroes trying to overcome formidable obstacles, and its atmosphere of strangeness and mystery. But unlike a few of the characters in that book, Wilson never lost his pleasure in the romance of the pursuit.

WILSON'S MODERNISM

DAVID BROMWICH

FOR READERS like me, who came to the older writers
by way of the moderns, Edmund Wilson's essays were
a great stimulus—a provocation and an incitement
to an interest in literature. Other critics one came to
later would matter more to one's sense of what critical
thought might be and the way a distinctive taste could
be expressed. But even as one got to know these
critics—Empson, Jarrell, and others—and read and reread them to try to see how they saw what they saw,
Wilson was in the background, and this was a comfort:
there was always more of him to read. He made a
good ground note for criticism, with a continuous intelligent levelness of style that ought to be an attainable ideal, except that nobody else close to our time
has attained it. His instrument was a prose very flexible
in the middle range of description, exposition, and
judgment, rather less flexible in giving the tactile or
sensuous character of a book. There were gifted formal
and didactic critics then, Blackmur and Tate for
example, whom one would never go to expecting a

translatable summary of anything, or an answerable
argument. His gifts, normal as he made them seem,
were unique.

Wilson's style is almost without heights, though it
can rise to a somber dignity in characterizing those personal heroes of his, in art or history, about whom he
makes one feel that single-minded enterprise may be a
source of passion. This feeling is strongest—close to
what the neoclassical writers called panegyric—in certain climactic descriptions of Proust and Marx. There
are no unplanned exuberances in his writing, no enthusiasms which he discloses without being able to account for, and almost no purple patches. Samuel
Johnson said that whenever a writer composed a sentence he thought particularly fine, he should blot it
immediately; and Wilson is one of the few critics in
English in this century who sound as if he wrote with
that rule in mind.

To characterize him as a *journalistic* critic has been
a usual tactic of academic condescension. But the
traits I mentioned do seem related to his having entered critical writing from the position of an editor,
mindful of the duties one may wrongly suppose to be
confined to the editorial part of journalism. He has an
excellent essay from the 1930s, an essay which has not
dated at all, called "The Literary Worker's Polonius,"
which speaks of the relations between editors and authors, editors and their periodical audience, and more
particularly of the responsibilities of the reviewer,
which were not in his view distinct from the responsibilities of the critic:

The reviewer, at the very least, should be expected to supply information. The retelling of the
story of a novel, the summary of an historical or
philosophical book, is the most boring part of the
reviewer's business, but it is an absolutely essential part. The reader should be given a chance to
judge whether or not he would be interested in
the book, irrespective of what the reviewer may
think of it; and it is an indispensable discipline for
the reviewer, or any critic, to give the gist of the
book in his own words. The reviewer, when he
sets about this task, is quite likely to find that there
is more in the book, or less in it, or something different in it, than he imagined when he first went
through it. If the author is incoherent or woolly,
the critic will be able to detect it. If the reviewer
is incompetent, his incompetence will be evident
to his more acute readers when they find out he
cannot tell them what is in the book.

Whatever other praise might be owed him, Wilson
would always have wanted to be thought a competent
reviewer in this sense, in the opinion of his more acute
readers. One reason the controversy about his review
of Nabokov's translation of *Eugene Onegin* came to
be so drawn out may have been his suspicion that he
had for once there exposed himself to a doubt among
those readers.

If we want a writer to compare him with, it had better be a figure of Victorian size and substance, on the
order of Leslie Stephen. I don't know that Wilson

cherished loyalties as intense as Stephen's were for the
authors—Darwin, Wordsworth, Butler, Burke, and a
few others—who he felt had taught him to reason about
"man, the heart of man, and human life," and there is
no single work by Wilson as centrally occupied with
the definition of his culture and its antecedents as were
Stephen's books on the English utilitarians and on
eighteenth-century English thought. And yet, in teaching the growth of historical materialism as a doctrine of
political theory and action, and the convergence of
symbolism and realism in the formation of modern literature, Wilson was carrying out a project at once as
public-minded and as inward as Stephen's when he
wrote of the passage from natural theology to the naturalism of evolutionary theory. With the mention of politics and literature, I may seem to conflate two phases of
work that do not properly belong together in Wilson's
career. But his explanation of the motives and technique of modernist literature in the '20s, and of the passage of socialism from thought to action in the '30s,
were undertakings less distinct in his mind than he and
his readers were apt to remember later on.

There is a revealing paragraph near the end of *Axel's
Castle*, in which Wilson speculates that

the time is at hand when these writers, who have
largely dominated the literary world of the decade
1920–30, though we shall continue to admire
them as masters, will no longer serve us as
guides. . . . In America the comfortable enjoyment
of what was supposed to be American prosperity,
which since the war had made it possible for

Americans to accept with a certain complacency the despondency as well as the resignation of European books, has given way to a sudden disquiet. And Americans and Europeans are both becoming more and more conscious of Russia, a country where a central social and political idealism has been able to use and to inspire the artist as well as the engineer. The question begins to press us as to whether it is possible to make a practical success of human society, and whether, if we continue to fail, a few masterpieces, however profound or noble, will be able to make life worth living even for the few people in a position to enjoy them.

A writer with contemporary aims as definite as this passage implies was required to be not just a competent but an imposing digester of doctrine; the producer, again and again, of the conspectus or synthesis that is accurate but not impartially intended. And a curious feature of Wilson's historical manner is the practice by which, quite often, to gather and concentrate excitement, he shifts the narration of a life into the present tense. It is a Homeric technique (as well as an effective lecturer's device)—an appropriate tactic in a writer interested, as he was, in catching the accent of the past as it carries into the present.

His two best-known books of criticism, *Axel's Castle* and *The Wound and the Bow*, imply a single story about modernism. The passive intensification of experience, which Wilson associates with an aristocratic character like Axel, has its counterpart in the defection from soci-

ety of an avant-garde poet like Rimbaud. These perso-
nae, one from fiction and one from life, represent a split
between reflection and action that started a century
earlier; and *Axel's Castle* asserts a strong connection
between romanticism and the moderns, Yeats, Valéry,
Stein, Joyce, Proust, and Eliot, with whom Wilson is
mainly concerned. It becomes possible to forget this in
reading the separate chapters, partly because Wilson's
idiom of description and praise is what we have come
to call modernist. His appreciation of the closing stanza
of "Among School Children" is not markedly different
from what one may find, in similar stretches of formal
summary, in a critic like Robert Penn Warren:

> Here the actual scene in the convent, the personal
> emotions it awakens and the general speculations
> which these emotions suggest, have been inter-
> woven and made to play upon each other at the
> same time that they are kept separate and distinct.
> A complex subject has been treated in the most
> concentrated form, and yet without confusion.
> Perceptions, fancies, feelings and thoughts all
> have their place in the poet's record. It is a mo-
> ment of human life, masterfully seized and made
> permanent, in all its nobility and lameness, its
> mystery and actuality, its direct personal contact
> and abstraction.

What is valued is the way a mood of meditation has
created sufficient detachment from a quite particular
represented moment. The demand, as in Warren's criticism, is that the poem be imaginable as the utterance
of a speaker in a situation—that it be seen to answer for

each constituent of the scene in order to earn credit for the dramatic urgency it imputes to a single speaker.

Often, in Wilson, the concern with representative adequacy joins a mood of exhilaration he seems to share with the authors he writes about, as if they were conspirators in a larger movement of thought and feeling. The mood is plain in his account of the dissatisfaction Paul Valéry must have felt with the whole tendency of established letters evoked by the name of Anatole France. "It was time," says Wilson, justifying Valéry's tone of repudiation, "that those formulas should be discarded—there was nothing more to be done along those lines. And Valéry is one of those who have abolished them." This is the note of modernist solidarity. But in working out its application, Wilson tends to return rather narrowly to the interest of techniques, as if they themselves changed the horizon of art. *Axel's Castle* concludes, on another hint from Valéry, with the question whether "as science and art look more and more deeply into experience and achieve a wider and wider range, and as they come to apply themselves more and more directly and expertly to the needs of human life, they may not arrive at a way of thinking, a technique of dealing with our perceptions, which will make science and art one." This sounds closer to Wells or Shaw than to Valéry, but the unifying aspiration could be heard at the time from writers not of the Wells-Shaw school. Eliot's obscurely programmatic essay "*Ulysses*, Order, and Myth" aims in a similar way at recruiting the techniques of art as instruments for adapting science to human ends. As one canvasses statements like these by Eliot and

Wilson and Valéry, one is surprised in retrospect by a certain lack of skepticism. For it is what artists exclude that defines a movement in art, much more than the ends they hope to achieve. In fact, the motifs of exclusion may be identical with those of innovation—they reveal something happening freshly in certain works which don't yet have a reason for it. Godard's first dozen films, and a phase of Ashbery's poetry, around the time of *Rivers and Mountains* and *The Double Dream of Spring*, were experiments of this kind that incidentally brought out new techniques: the jump cut, which moviegoers first saw in *Breathless*, was a contraction of the syntax of montage as inspired as the off-center cropping of limbs in Degas's pictures of dancers. The style of ellipsis that Ashbery employed to suggest an atmosphere of feeling both nostalgic and abstract was a step away from the foreshortened evocations of time and place in "The Fire Sermon." The invention carries its own morality which people feel as part of the motive of the new work, without the artist's having to answer for it. When the artist does try to say what his style was up to all along, the result is apt to be obvious, evasive, and minimal, as in Eliot's critical pronouncements on verse drama, or dogmatic in a self-betraying way, as in the face-the-camera soliloquies of Godard's films of the late '60s. This degree of explicitness seems a fault when we see it in a work of art. It is not less so in criticism, and Wilson, in general, seems to me to have been too keen to appeal from the sensations of the work to its palpable design. Adorno, a modernist less trustful of artists and methods who set more store by the work, wrote with summary accuracy: "In every work of art something appears that does not exist." He had in mind, among other things, that sense of projected purpose that a work may show without saying, a purpose that teaches over the head of the author. Wilson allowed for such a possibility, too; but wherever he could, he brought the meanings of the work back to rest in the experience of the author.

This included, of course, unconscious experience. *The Wound and the Bow*, in its remarkable chapters on Dickens and Kipling, treats the artist's *oeuvre* as a coherent entity and the life of the artist as a story with a single burden. These studies rely on the intuition that the specialization and stress of genius may be consequences of a traumatic experience that evades analysis. Psychoanalytic mechanisms such as displacement and projection would seem to have a place in this account, which adapts Freud's general understanding of art as sublimation. But the sense one may retain from a distance, that the argument of *The Wound and the Bow* is somehow psychoanalytic, turns out to be hard to justify in the presence of the book. When Freud wrote about the imagination, he was interested in the contrast between manifest and latent content, between the repressed and what is available for representation. By contrast, Wilson takes as his subject the affective or physical weakness and strength of certain writers, and their life and work are treated as of a piece. The critic brings to light what may have been elusive, not in the space between the work and the artist but between the artist's public and private identities. The "wound" that

draws the identities into coherence is a private injury,
intelligible in normative terms, which the artist has
turned to mysterious advantage. I think that the idea of
a kind of unconscious activity peculiar to art was alien
to Wilson. This may explain his curious error in sup-
posing that the Yeatsian idea of the antithetical self was
a discipline the artist could impose on himself rather
than a disturbing and negative affinity by which the artist was chosen as if from outside.

Little as Wilson borrows or seems to have learned
from the romantic sense of the mind as an unconscious
power, in *The Wound and the Bow* he brings to his
analysis of modern writers a version of the romantic
idea of genius. He expounds his moral from the story of
the Philoctetes of Sophocles: "The victim of a malodor-
ous disease which renders him abhorrent to society and
periodically degrades him and makes him helpless is
also the master of a superhuman art which everybody
has to respect and which the normal man finds he
needs." It is not clear from any of the chapters on what
ground the normal man—assuming him to be part of
the audience as well as part of the subject of modern
art—may enter into relation with the hidden, humiliat-
ing, and (as the normal mind regards them) repulsive
sufferings which have here been so intimately associated with art. Wilson's language works hard throughout
the book to assimilate to a normal idiom whatever may
seem dangerous in the sickness of the artist: he speaks
not of neurosis or repression but of "obsession," of
"morbid" excess and "breakdown," and remarks with a
matter-of-fact analogical assurance in the chapter on
Kipling: "While the locomotives and airplanes and

steamers were beating records and binding continents, the human engine was going wrong. The age of mechanical technique was also the age of the nerve sanitarium." The hopeful suggestion that humanity is on a wrong path which art can show the reasons of, or that, to paraphrase Shelley, at moments of social decay art sympathizes with the decay, is not in fact borne out in the texture of the individual studies. While their aggregate moral comes from Sophocles, the epigraph that gives the book its title is from Joyce: "I bleed by the black stream for my torn bough"—a confession, once more, of the isolation of the artist, which leads back to suffering and to the refinement of the idiosyncrasies of art. Joyce's words echo the words Hazlitt used to describe the aberrant hero of Godwin's *St. Leon*: "He is a limb torn from society."

The apparent premise of Wilson's early criticism, and of much of the modernist criticism that followed, is not that the artist is isolated and the results of the isolation somehow interesting. Nor is it that the artist may be representative and exceptional at once. Instead, we are asked to grant that the anomaly and the inwardness of art are a condition of the exemplary humanity of its maker. This seems to me an enormous weight to ask the artist to bear. It also implies a trust more wisely given to the work than the author, but Wilson's appeal in these books goes steadily in the other direction, from the quality of a poem or book to the pathos that the life of its author can be felt to possess.

His emphasis is most credible in the chapter on Hemingway, a writer about whom he always wrote with great impartiality and intelligence:

Ideas, however correct, will never prevail by themselves: there must be people who are prepared to stand or fall with them, and the ability to act on principle is still subject to the same competitive laws which operate in sporting contests and sexual relations. Hemingway has expressed with genius the terrors of modern man at the danger of losing control of his world, and he has also, within his scope, provided his own kind of antidote. This antidote, paradoxically, is almost entirely moral. Despite Hemingway's preoccupation with physical contests, his heroes are almost always defeated physically, nervously, practically: their victories are moral ones. He himself, when he trained himself stubbornly in his unconventional unmarketable art in a Paris which had other fashions, gave the prime example of such a victory; and if he has sometimes, under the menace of the general panic, seemed on the point of going to pieces as an artist, he has always pulled himself together the next moment.

Thus, the artist, while he achieves his own moral victory, becomes a hero of resistance by gaining credence for the power of the ideas he wants to make prevail. Strangely, for a critic whose reputation linked an interest in literature with an interest in society, Wilson never saw the work of art as involved in a relation to society that would make for some other aesthetic task than that of bearing the advanced ideas or incorporating the advanced techniques.

A sense of the heroism of the writer, centered on the experiments of Eliot and Joyce and Valéry, was bound to exhibit the spirit of vanguardism in a way something like this. Wilson in *Axel's Castle* and *The Wound and the Bow* was a sharer in the common modernist hope of joining aesthetic with moral reflection, which led naturally enough, in him as in other critics, to the hope of binding social progress to aesthetic change. The only account of modern art that may feel more satisfactory is one that surrenders this aspiration, with a prudential or dandyish retraction of hope that runs a risk of complacency. I have in mind Baudelaire's argument—more a stance than an argument—in "The Painter of Modern Life." As Baudelaire saw it, the absorption in sheer surfaces by which the modern artist performed his work might open for reflection the feelings of arbitrary excitement that drive everyday life in modernity. In critics fairly close to Wilson's generation, this different feeling for the new could lead to a recognition that dandyism has its own integrity for the artist; as in a characteristic aphorism by Harold Rosenberg on the supposed method of modern art: "He loiters in the neighborhood of a problem. After a while a solution strolls by." The task of art on this view is identical with the task of discovering the present. One's materials and methods are uncertain, and practitioners must cleave with an unsentimental fidelity to the surface effects of fashion. "If it wants to avoid selling out," as Adorno remarks, "art has to resist fashion while simultaneously internalizing it." The process of internalization is interesting in itself, and can yield thoughts discrete from

Wilson's about some of the authors he cared for, like Eliot, and some, like Beckett, of whom he had little or nothing to say. A preoccupied concern with internalizing fashion may lead to compulsive externalization as well, plainly enough in evidence in theories of post-modernism, and in the works executed obedient to those theories. Wilson was a heroic historian of the resistance to fashion by the artist, and the part of the truth he tells is the part most apt to be neglected now.

THE WRITER'S EYE

JED PERL

EDMUND WILSON believed that his classical verbal precision was equal to any occasion, and he made his point with a shelf full of books that are so clearheaded and wide-ranging that they leave us exhilarated. Considering the magisterial egotism at work here, it's not surprising that there have always been readers tempted to respond to Wilson's omnivorousness by poking around for the areas that he slighted or overlooked. And that's by no means the end of the story. Ever the intellectual competitor, Wilson wanted to stay a few steps ahead of even the most demanding readers by locating and repairing the gaps in his own ambitiously comprehensive view. In 1963, when he wrote "Every Man His Own Eckermann"—a mock interview, really a comic playlet—for the fledgling *New York Review of Books*, he was casually displaying his grasp of exactly the subjects that people felt were not up his alley, such as nineteenth-century comic illustration and Stravinsky's chamber music. Here was a man who was even at home with the material he wasn't supposed to know.

As this dialogue begins, a fictional visitor, associated with the new magazine, presses Wilson to give his opinion on "all the arts. . . . That's what I wanted to ask you about. You've written so much about literature but not much about painting and music. We wondered if you wouldn't contribute some opinions about graphic and musical subjects." Wilson is testing the limits of his intellectual reach, so with mock modesty he responds, "Gladly: I know nothing whatever about them." Yet the visitor is quick to point out that the eminent author hasn't completely overlooked the other arts. "In the twenties you used to do articles on concerts and exhibitions." That, Wilson replies, was when he was a "cultural man-of-all-work" for the *New Republic*: "I wrote about everything from burlesque shows and circuses to Stravinsky and Georgia O'Keeffe. I'd never dare to write such stuff today." And here he is, forty years later, writing just "such stuff."

"Every Man His Own Eckermann" is one of Wilson's self-consciously amused self-portraits as a bookish old man. Yet even as he's deliciously casting himself in a role, he manages to speak with some passion about his affinity for the graphic arts, which he dates all the way back to the engravings by Callot that he bought in France when serving in World War I. Wilson then launches into a list of graphic artists who interest him. He says he likes "picture books in general of the comic or fantastic kind: Gilray, Rowlandson, Fuseli, Spitzweg, Cruickshank, Phiz, Edward Lear, Beardsley, Toulouse-Lautrec, George du Maurier, Phil May, Max Beerbohm, Sem, Max Ernst, Marc Chagall, Peggy Bacon, Saul Steinberg, Leonard Baskin, Edward Gorey—to mention people of very different magnitudes." He describes his passion for the turn-of-the-century caricaturist Sem, and makes a point of comparing Sem's interpretations of various late-nineteenth-century figures with those of his friend and contemporary, Proust; he observes that the delicate storytelling in the illustrations of Henri Monnier anticipates elements in Flaubert and Maupassant; and he speaks at length of his enthusiasm for George Grosz.

Wilson likes pictures with a strong narrative or anecdotal dimension, and that's to be expected in a literary man. His taste in music also runs to works with words and plots; in the self-interview he focuses on opera and gets into a discussion of the relationship between Mussorgsky and Pushkin. It's disappointing to find him taking a greater interest in the clever anecdotes of Tchelitchew than in the graphic elaborations of Picasso, but Tchelitchew is an enthusiasm he shares with Lincoln Kirstein and other people who ought to know better. Too much can be made of the idiosyncracies in Wilson's taste; what's really impressive is his endless curiosity. In "Every Man His Own Eckermann" he even has ideas about the work that he doesn't care for at all, so that you feel him bringing the same front-and-center attention to art and music that he'd at one time or another brought to foreign cities and popular culture, as well as to literature and history.

In spite of Wilson's somewhat dismissive remarks about his journalism of the '20s—some of which was written for *Vanity Fair*, where he was managing editor in 1920—he never lost his early appetite for pictures and music. There are a number of fascinating twists to

this interest in the nonliterary arts, not the least of
which is that the narrator of his most important work of
fiction, *Memoirs of Hecate County*, is an art critic whose
life in many respects parallels Wilson's. This man is not
an Edmund Wilson self-portrait; this is a portrait of a
man who would like to be the kind of writer that
Wilson was but lacks the focused energy necessary to
pull his artistic and economic interests together into a
Wilsonian whole. Yet there are pages in *Hecate County*
where one feels that Wilson is enjoying seeing things
through the eyes of this aesthete—recording the way
that a connoisseur mentally catalogues the Canova and
Daubigny and Corot in one suburban home, or analyzing the art-historical inspirations behind the various
dresses worn by Imogen Loomis, the Princess with the
Golden Hair whom the narrator pursues through the
central story in the book.

Wilson, the man who wears so many literary hats,
can't resist imagining himself as a critic in an entirely
different field. In an unfinished novel, written before
Hecate County—it's scheduled for publication under
the title *The Higher Jazz*—the narrator is a would-be
composer rather than an art critic, and you feel Wilson
rising to the challenge of yet another form. Here he describes the man's feelings at the beginning of a performance of Schoenberg's *Pierrot Lunaire*: "Schoenberg
had always gotten me and he still did. It was partly
the Wagner that was still behind it, though all reduced
to moonlight and blackness, discolored and flattened
out—the old thrill of the Germanic music theater, the
shiver and the shudder and the longing ache." The ex-

pansive yet precise language is vintage Wilson. No matter what the subject, he is himself. In *Hecate County*, when the narrator reflects on the inadequacy of Clive Bell's formalism, we can see that Wilson is spinning a variation on his basic point of view, which is that it's always useful to set literature in a broad cultural context. In both *The Higher Jazz* and *Hecate County*, Wilson is drawing on his experience at *Vanity Fair*, and it's clear that his early immersion in the everything-is-new days of modern art had implications that went way beyond the confines of literature and stayed with him for a very long time.

In *The American Earthquake* (1958), which Wilson subtitled *A Documentary of the Twenties and Thirties*, articles about Alfred Stieglitz's gallery and some recent compositions by Stravinsky are printed one after the other. In the Stieglitz piece, Wilson writes admiringly about Georgia O'Keeffe's flower abstractions, comments on works by Dove, Marin, and Hartley, and concludes with a beautiful description of Stieglitz's recent cloud photographs, the *Equivalents*. In the Stravinsky article—actually two notices joined together—he describes the Piano Concerto of 1924 and *Petrushka*, and touches on work by Schoenberg, Varèse, and Satie. These pieces—together with a review of a George Bellows exhibition at the Metropolitan Museum of Art— evince an extraordinary ease and authority in writing about arts other than literature.

In the Stravinsky review, Wilson speaks about the echoes of Handel and Bach in the new Octet and Concerto, saying that in the Piano Concerto "the Bachesque development is finally broken up by momentary ragtime rhythms and fragments of sarcastic parody, just as Eliot interrupts his Elizabethan blank verse with bar talk and popular songs." The comparison isn't noteworthy in itself—it's a fairly standard observation about the modernist mingling of the classical and everyday—but there's something about the unforced, I'm-making-this-just-in-passing demeanor of the writing that underlines the directness of his response to a nonliterary subject. His emotions on hearing a piece of music or seeing a photograph can be as immediate as his feelings about a book. I wonder if anybody has ever bettered his description of the Stieglitz cloud studies. He writes:

> Stieglitz, in pushing his mastery of the camera further and further from mechanical reproduction and closer to the freedom of plastic art, has lately left the earth altogether and taken to the shifting clouds, where he seems to have found a material of maximum variability. The textures and shapes of the sky are infinitely irregular and strange, and they never are twice the same—so that the artist can have practically whatever he likes; and the person who looks at the picture is never distracted from the artist's intention by recognizing familiar objects, familiar subjects of photographs. One finds effects of a feathery softness or of a solidity almost marmoreal. Certain of these prints, I suppose, are among the artist's chief triumphs. Especially impressive are cloud-masses—somber and grand in their darkness—which lift themselves as if in grief.

The marmoreal clouds, by the way, reappear in the chapter on Valéry in *Axel's Castle*.

When Wilson gathered some of these early nonliterary pieces in *The American Earthquake*, he wrote postscripts to the Stieglitz and Stravinsky articles in which he saluted the two men, pointing to them as heroic figures. After noting Stieglitz's steely control and unwillingness to brook disagreement, Wilson adds that he "commanded respect. To think that he had been working for 'modern' art—in an age of convention and commerce—since the time when I was ten years old!" The '20s had been, as Wilson reported in later years, a complicated time for him, exhilarating but also exhausting and demoralizing, closing with the crisis that he described as "a kind of" nervous breakdown. From the vantage point of the '50s, he remarked that "it touches me today to think of [Stieglitz] running counter to the pressures of that era and trying to make beauty of—in Paul Rosenfeld's words—the 'strange brazen human emptiness' of the city in which I then lived." As for Stravinsky, if in 1925 Wilson sounded a bit lukewarm about the recent work of a composer who was in mid-career, with what is generally regarded as his greatest work behind him, succeeding decades led the critic to revise that judgment: "I have come to respect and prize him even more highly than I did thirty years ago when he was still a novel excitement. His intensity and variety, his persistence and craftsmanship, continue to delight and to fortify the worker in any craft." These views on Stravinsky are repeated, in a slightly different form, in "Every Man His Own Eckermann," where Wilson praises the "sustained career" and how Stra-

vinsky is "always himself and always doing something
different, but always doing everything intensely with
economy, perfect craftsmanship and style."

A fellow critic and close friend of Wilson's whose
words and thoughts are woven into these writings on
both Stieglitz and Stravinsky is Paul Rosenfeld. Wilson
had begun to read Rosenfeld's music criticism "with
avidity" even before he met him in 1922—the year of
The Waste Land and *Ulysses*—and for Wilson Rosenfeld held a key to the American Renaissance, for he was
close to the Stieglitz circle and wrote about all the
arts. In later years, Rosenfeld came to represent for
Wilson the part of the '20s that hadn't been about
drinking and wild parties but about a questing artistic
and intellectual spirit. Rosenfeld personified "the new
era of American art [that was] just beginning to burst
into life between MacDougal Street and Irving Place."
It is from him that Wilson borrowed the phrase about
Stieglitz's relationship with New York, and in both the
1925 piece on Stravinsky and the postscript, Wilson
quoted an interview that Rosenfeld had conducted
with Stravinsky and published in the *Dial*, in which
the Russian announced that, although there was much
to envy about the situation of the musician in Bach's
day, "I feel we in our day are working with our material
in the spirit of Bach, the constructive spirit, and I feel
that what we give, though it is perhaps smaller in
comparison, is in its concentration and economy an
equivalent for the immense structures of Bach." For
Wilson there was something compelling about the
range of Paul Rosenfeld's interests—he was against
narrow specialization, a believer in intellectual versatil-

THE WRITER'S EYE   61

ity. Like Wilson he was not a card-carrying member of
the modern movement but a dedicated observer,
whose avidity enabled him to bring the modern news
to a growing public.

Wilson, who is sometimes thought, and not without
reason, to have been a sort of Edwardian figure, had a
keen eye for the musical and visual expressions of the
new century. He could evoke modern taste quickly and
wittily, as in this 1927 description of a fictional Greenwich Village apartment, with its precise, bare-bones
decor. "On the white walls, above the row of book-
shelves, were brass candlesticks with red candles in
them, an oval daguerreotype of a rugged Wyoming
grandfather, a black bowl of red holly-berries, an Alas-
kan illustration that Rockwell Kent had given her and
two portraits of herself—one a charcoal drawing and
the other a painting that presented her with green skin
and half-shut eyes and made her look like a corpse."
This is the apartment of a character named Jane Gooch,
editor of a magazine called *Vortex*, which is planning,
we are told, "a big hydraulic number." This, Gooch explains, will focus on "pipes and oil pumps and plumb-
ing fixtures—and all those things. We've got some
photographs of bathrooms by Leo Kleist that are the
most marvellous things you ever saw. There's a series—of wash-basins at different angles—that looks just
like the tomb of the Medicis."

This is a wonderful send-up of the kind of willfully
abstract photography that was already becoming a
cliché in the '20s. That Wilson's parody is so perfectly
on target reflects an insider's understanding; and elsewhere in his writing he himself uses for serious literary

effect the very eye for abstraction that he's joking about here. He grasps the transforming power of simplification and exaggeration; it was a technique that was being passed back and forth between the writers and the painters throughout this period. Take, for example, his description of the apartment of the Dimiceli family in Brooklyn, in a piece of reportage from the early '30s that's called "A Bad Day in Brooklyn":

> The Dimicelis' flat is extremely clean, and it is furnished with an unexpected vividness that contrasts with the discolored streets of Flushing. The walls of every room are decorated with bright religious prints in green, blue and red—the Bleeding Heart and the Holy Family, the Virgin with flowers in her arms that presides above the bed in the bedroom, the Last Supper over the kitchen table. The whole apartment, in fact, has the brightness and the clear outlines of one of those simple prints: bedroom walls in green, kitchen oilcloth in blue and white squares, kitchen curtains in green and white, kitchen table and sink smooth white, and three yellow canaries in yellow cages.

Wilson's description represents the same hyperrefined, aestheticized documentary sensibility that we recognize in the photographs Walker Evans was beginning to take around the same time. In their essential spirit, both men hark back to what, in *Axel's Castle*, Wilson called Flaubert's "aesthetic Naturalism." But his use of primary and secondary colors also gives the writing some of the daring, immediate simplicity that painters achieved early in the century by avoiding halftones and shadows. He almost turns the Dimiceli home into an interior by Matisse. Wilson has a modern feeling for the freestanding descriptive power of words. Think of the title of one of his collections of travel writings— *Red, Black, Blond and Olive*, his studies of Zuñi, Haitian, Soviet, and Israeli culture. He sends those names of colors, with their complicated metaphoric implications, into the world with all the stark, mysterious elegance of Rimbaud's, *"A noir, E blanc, I rouge, U vert, O bleu."* And, of course, *Axel's Castle* concludes with Rimbaud.

Even the design of Wilson's books, with their distinctive size and superbly elegant typographic covers, underlines the feeling that the modern movement gives words a new kind of lucidity and power. No other twentieth-century American writer imposed so firm a design sense on a range of publishers over a long period of years. I think there can be little doubt that it's Wilson himself who inspired the equally brilliant dust jackets done by Ivan Chermayeff for *The American Earthquake* at Doubleday and by Ronald Clyne for *Wilson's Night Thoughts* at Farrar, Straus, Cudahy. And then there's Edward Gorey's comic but elegant design for *The Duke of Palermo and Other Plays*. Wilson's feeling for typographic clarity unites two styles that dominated the book arts in the '20s. In these extraordinarily designed covers, there's a merger of the sophisticated traditionalist approach of the '20s, with its return to an eighteenth-century severity and simplicity, and the very different but equally vigorous constructivist graphic style that was being developed by modernists in Germany and Holland.

Wilson had a wonderful eye, and it gives descriptive
power to everything from his snapshots of the shabby
Finland Station, all "rubber-gray and tarnished pink,"
in the closing pages of his "Study in the Writing and
Acting of History," to a description of Punch and Judy
puppets, with their brilliant colors, in his travel diary
from the 1963 trip to Europe. His descriptive gift is
grounded, as is the psychological genius of his portraits
of writers, in an insistence on seeing everything whole
and clear. All of Wilson's intellectual powers gain concrete form through the beautifully regular rhythm of
his prose, with each word presented exactly, precisely,
so that we seem to take its full measure before we pass
onto the next word. It's thrilling when this dense, eloquent voice, apparently so well suited for discussions of
books, takes on subjects as unexpected as the architecture of Thomas Jefferson and the prints of John James
Audubon in a chapter on poetry in *Patriotic Gore*.
Wilson speaks of Jefferson's University of Virginia, and
with what "sure a touch [he] has situated his charming
creations on the hospitable little hills in such as way as
to involve the landscape in a personal work of art. The
bubble domes, the candid facades, the variety of the
classical cornices in the 'pavilions' that enclose the university 'lawn' and in which the professors live, the delightful white octagon rooms, with French windows
that open on level vistas, have humanized the Palladian
style into something eclectic and lovely." What a surprising adjective that *candid* is. In Audubon's studies of
quadrupeds Wilson admires "his genius for personaliz-
ing and dramatizing his subjects and, by the imaginative use of landscape, embodying them in balanced

compositions." Here is "the magnificent striped plume of the mother skunk defending from the vantage of a hollow log her still groping babies inside it." And "the violet rosettes of the star-nosed moles that delicately vibrate to their prey in the darkness of the burrows or streams where they hunt" and make "a strange contrast with the free-skimming sails on the river in the distance behind them."

You might think that by the time of *Patriotic Gore*— published in 1962—after the decades of politics and reportage, Wilson would have little appetite for the visual flexibility necessary to make such delicate discriminations within the work of an architect or a watercolorist, yet in the lines on Jefferson's architecture and Audubon's animals he shows the same acute visual sense that he'd brought to Stieglitz's gallery decades before. It's an amazing passage in *Patriotic Gore*—there's a sense of looking up from the thick rows of nineteenth-century memoirs that loom so large in Wilson's Civil War work, up to the landscape, and that expansion of the horizon somehow recalls the way Stieglitz, in his cloud studies, looks up from what's ordinary to take in a wider, immediately surprising view. The elegant severity of Wilson's mind did not allow for a more consistently expansive exploration of interconnections between the arts, but this did not mean that he was indifferent or unsympathetic to such associations. On the contrary, much as in the '20s he had admired Rosenfeld's willingness to take the risk of interweaving the arts, in his later years Wilson was praising writers, especially André Malraux and Mario Praz, who felt equally at home in literature and the visual arts.

In 1951 Wilson published a review of the first three volumes of Malraux's extended exploration of art history. And when he reprinted the essay in *The Bit Between My Teeth* in 1965, he added a long afterword, discussing the volumes that had flowed from these early ones and that together struck him as forming a lavishly illustrated "kind of huge philosophic prose poem." Malraux's spiraling narrative comes out of the studio atmosphere of early-twentieth-century Paris, where the artists had been eager to relate their work to the heretofore ignored or misunderstood masterpieces of Romanesque and African and Asian civilization. Malraux threads his opulent, almost stream-of-consciousness, approach to the history of art through pages full of beautifully lit, dramatically cropped photographs, photographs that in some respects are related to the unexpected close-up views Wilson was parodying in the piece on Jane Gooch and her *Vortex* magazine. Yet he takes immediately to Malraux's layered vision, to the way that whole epochs and continents are interwoven and crosscut to get at the feeling of open access to the past that you so often feel in the studios of modern artists, where reproductions are tacked to the walls and books are brought out to give visitors a broad context for what the artist is doing now.

Malraux, he writes, "skips all over Europe from one cathedral to another, and from these to illuminated Psalters and Books of Hours and the works of art in palaces and mansions, and this involves an adroit play of mind which must dart here and there in both space and time to show analogies and point up contrasts." Wilson goes into Malraux's spinning, cycling universe

with some of the avidity that he'd given to another
product of modern art's ripeness, Joyce's *Finnegans
Wake*; his review of Malraux has some of the combination of overall enthusiasm plus reservations that he'd
brought to his discussions of the later Joyce. He compares the book to Gibbon, Tolstoy, and Marx. In response to those who would criticize Malraux for attempting too much, he asks, "Is not Malraux himself an
artist who, whether working in terms of the history of
art or of fiction based on current history, has, by the
force of imagination, been recreating for us our world?"
Wilson was on friendly terms with Malraux; they had in
common the experience of literary men who'd been immersed in the political hopes of the century, and at the
end of the day they both perhaps were coming back to
the way they'd felt in the beginning, when the freestanding integrity of a work of art was the most important thing of all.

By saluting Malraux's history of art Wilson was also
reaffirming his sympathy for the modern collaging of
many historical styles that we find in Eliot and Pound
and Joyce, even if he had expressed a certain hesitancy
about what he described as their "veritable literary mu-
seums." Another enthusiasm of Wilson's later years, for
the writings of Mario Praz, brought with it precious
midcentury echoes of the fin de siècle colorations of
those other figures out of *Axel's Castle*, Yeats and
Proust. We know that the first and last pieces in
Wilson's literary chronicles have each been chosen
very carefully, and have a particular personal significance. *Classics and Commercials*—the chronicle of the
'40s—ends with Wilson's fine-grained memoir of Paul

Rosenfeld. *The Bit Between My Teeth*, covering the years 1950–65, ends with a long article about Praz, the Italian writer who was as interested in the visual arts as he was in literature. Earlier in *The Bit Between My Teeth* is a review of the book of Praz's that's still best known in America, his study of the influence of de Sade on the romantics called *The Romantic Agony*. The essay on Praz with which the book concludes, much larger in scope, is an attempt to give American readers a sense of the whole range of Praz's concerns.

Wilson focuses on Praz's autobiography, *The House of Life*, which takes the form of a room-by-room tour of his apartment on the Via Giulia in Rome—thus the title of the essay, "The Genie of the Via Giulia." This autobiography is in part the confession of an obsessive collector of neoclassical and Empire antiques; but each object that catches Praz's eye, whether it's a dark mahogany bookcase with bronze fittings, or a watercolor of a Neopolitan interior, or a series of porcelain plates depicting scenes along the Thames, inspires such a stream of asides and memories that the whole book takes on a Proustian psychological fascination. Wilson speaks of his visits to Praz's home, where he was "made to feel that there were presences lurking about me." And he goes on to say, "These presences—artists long passed into eclipse, craftsmen no longer famous, vanished families, faded myths—have somehow been brought to life, refreshened by proximity to Mario Praz."

The House of Life is, like Malraux's symphonic writings on art—and like Paul Rosenfeld's salute to the American Renaissance, *Port of New York*—a work in which an eager appetite for images energizes a literary imagination. Wilson understood exactly what these writers were up to. When he responded with such wholeheartedness to *The House of Life*—calling it Praz's masterpiece—he must have felt, with a shiver of excitement, as if he were revisiting the tastes and enthusiasms he'd explored decades earlier, among the Symbolists of *Axel's Castle*. The richly figured surfaces and elegantly echoing distances of Praz's *House of Life* cannot but bring to mind elements in the writings of Pater and Huysmans and the Goncourt brothers. All this would have been obvious to Wilson. During their 1963–64 visit to Europe, Wilson and his wife Elena had dinner at Praz's apartment. In his diary Wilson noted that Elena was made "uncomfortable" by the proliferation of Praz's ponderous Empire furnishings; as for Wilson, he was delighted by this apartment overflowing with strange and rare and beautiful old things. Here was a nineteenth-century universe that had somehow survived, and Wilson was glad to turn away from the hard-edged brilliance of the modern movement that he'd begun to report on decades earlier, when he was a young man only recently home from the war.

EDMUND WILSON AND

GENTILE

PHILO-SEMITISM

◆

MARK KRUPNICK

INQUIRY INTO Edmund Wilson's ideas about the Jews
has led me to believe that Wilson's statements about
Jews tell as much about him as about their ostensible
subject. Turning to ancient Jewish history was a way
for this old-stock American, who had been reared as a
Presbyterian, to affirm his links to his ancestral tradition without affirming his ancestors' theology. Wilson
wound up identifying with the Jews as had his New
England Calvinist forebears. Thinking of himself as a
kind of Jew gave him a dignified alternative to what
seemed to him the cheapness and light-mindedness of
twentieth-century American culture.

Matthew Arnold's opposition of Hebraism and Hellenism remains a central topos of Western civilization.
The opposition of Athens and Jerusalem appears also in
the writings of Heinrich Heine, from whom it came
down to Arnold. Heine was concerned with real He-

brews, including himself insofar as he was torn between his Jewish origins and his ambition to be accepted as a European poet. But the "Hebraism" Arnold
had in mind was that of the English Nonconformists
who were his contemporaries. For Arnold, Hebraism
stood for strict observance of divine law, as embodied
in the English Puritan moral tradition. "Hellenism," its
opposite, stood for "culture" in what was for Arnold its
most positive sense, as the free play of the mind.

Wilson himself was an inheritor of the old Christian
way of thinking about Jews; that is, thinking typologi-
cally, figuratively, or in any other way that satisfied the
needs of Christian supersessionist apologetics. Like
Arnold, he had a "Hebraism" of his own. He started out
in the 1920s with many of the social prejudices characteristic of his upper-middle-class WASP background.
But Wilson transcended the limits of that culture in the
course of his lifetime. Unlike Matthew Arnold, he had
the chance to know many Jews. Most striking, in view
of the conventional prejudices of his social class and
his generation, Wilson usually liked the Jewish literary
intellectuals, academics, and publishers with whom he
rubbed elbows. Among the friends whose company he
most enjoyed were Isaiah Berlin, Daniel Aaron, Leon
Edel, Alfred Kazin, and Jason Epstein. What makes the
congeniality suprising is that Wilson's heyday, the period 1920–50, is often thought of as the age of T. S.
Eliot, who made Christian orthodoxy fashionable in literary studies and who famously thought too many free-
thinking Jews undesirable in an ideal Christian society.
The Jewish writers for whom Wilson served as a model
or mentor or just plain friend were usually deeply de-

voted. And with reason. It's hard to think of another
Anglo-American literary person of Wilson's time who
was as philo-Semitic as he.

That doesn't mean Wilson liked every Jew he met.
What he celebrated was a certain idea of the Jews. To
understand that idea we need to turn to Wilson's view
of his American-Calvinist inheritance and his conscious
effort, in the post-World War II period, to retrieve his
American spiritual legacy. We have to start with his
state of mind in the 1940s. Wilson had spent most of
the Depression years researching and writing *To the
Finland Station*, but by the time he had reached the
end of that book he had decisively turned against Marxism and lost most of his interest in socialism. Like many
other former leftists, he responded to his loss by turning inward. The evidence of that turning is *The Wound
and the Bow* (1941), a loosely "Freudian" book that
brings together seven essays on writers who had experienced emotional turmoil yet, like Sophocles' Philoctetes, found a compensating strength.

At the end of the war, Wilson toured a devastated
Europe and wrote a travel report, *Europe Without
Baedeker* (1947), which is remarkable for its *Schaden-
freude* over the drab, depressing, postwar scene. In addition to reaffirming his distaste for the British establishment, he was announcing the cultural bankruptcy
of Europe. The effect of two world wars was to persuade him that the Old World was quite as unregener-
ate as his American forebears had believed. Wilson
wrote much less about European subjects after 1945.
Although he continued to travel abroad, the last three
decades of his literary life mark a coming home. The

literary historian who had written pioneering studies of
Proust and Joyce turned now to the writing of Ambrose
Bierce and Mary Chesnut. The socialist who had admired Marx and Lenin in *To the Finland Station* devoted the 1950s to national heroes including Ulysses S.
Grant and Robert E. Lee. Even when Wilson did write
about non-American topics, his mood was retrospective. Typical of his last collection of essays, *The Bit
Between My Teeth* (1965), are the eccentric and "old-
fogeyish" (Wilson's word for himself in these years)
reconsiderations of minor, distinctly nonmodernist figures who had been popular in his youth. During his last
two decades, he also explored Western societies that
were dissident in relation to mainline culture and centralized governments. The travel book *Red, Black,
Blond and Olive* (1956) that succeeds *Europe Without
Baedeker* contains substantial sections on Haiti and
the Zuñi Indians of the American Southwest. Wilson
subsequently wrote entire books on marginalized
groups, like the Iroquois who used to roam the region
around his upstate New York family home, and the
French Canadians of Quebec. These are the years in
which he was most engaged with the Jews, who also
appear in his writing as a minority culture crushed by
successive imperial powers, down to the Nazis in our
time. Wilson studied the Jews partly to learn what had
enabled them to survive.

In *Patriotic Gore* he is the historian of the fate of
American Calvinism in the developments leading up
to the Civil War and in its aftermath. The question
to which he kept returning was this: How did old-
stock Americans, people like himself who had been

brought up on an older creed, adjust to the plutocratic
America that followed the Civil War? His Civil War
book occupied him on and off for about fifteen years.
Wilson shows a certain sympathy for the Old South,
which appears as yet another minority culture victim-
ized by the central state, but his major focus is on the
North, including the abolitionists, who provided what
he considered an ideological cover for the North's drive
for expansion. These sections on Northern writers like
Harriet Beecher Stowe allowed him to consider the
role of Calvinism in the abolitionist crusade and, by a
curious route, take up the ancient Israelite component
in New England Calvinism and in his own family's
tradition.

   This would seem to be an unusual way by which to
come to philo-Semitism. But of all the proud, dissenting groups Wilson praised in the postwar period, it was
the Jews who appear from his writing to have mattered
most. There are many threads in his romance with the
Jews. He writes in *Patriotic Gore* about the Old Testament scholar Calvin Ellis Stowe, the husband of Harriet Beecher, who so identified with the ancient Israelites that Harriet sometimes referred to him as "my poor
rabbi." Wilson himself was derived from the first New
England Puritans; Cotton Mather, like Calvin Stowe in
wearing a skullcap in his study, was a collateral ances-
tor. These early Americans, as Wilson frequently
pointed out, had thought of themselves as latter-day Israelites who had come to the New World as to Canaan.
"The Puritanism of New England," he writes, "was a
kind of new Judaism, a Judaism transposed into Anglo-
Saxon terms. These Protestants, in returning to the text

of the Bible, had concentrated on the Old Testament, and some had tried to take it as literally as any Ortho- dox Jews." Believing themselves to have been chosen by God for their "errand into the wilderness," the Puri- tans conceived their leaving England as a latter-day Exodus from Egyptian enslavement. In the New World, they felt themselves, like Abraham, to be bound in a covenant with God, and conducted themselves as if charged with being a light unto the nations.

One theme never explicitly spelled out but implicit in Wilson's autobiographical essays and in his bio- graphical portraits is that of chosenness. Although Wilson had no use for Calvinist theology, he retained, in a secularized form, a sense of having been marked for a special destiny. David Castronovo has pointed out that "Bible study and the pride of being set apart from less serious people were very definite features of [Wilson's] early life." He may have disliked his grand- mother's religious lessons when he was a boy, but his memoirs make clear his pride in a tradition that in- cluded successive generations of doctors and lawyers, including his own father, Edmund Wilson, Sr., who was attorney general of New Jersey when Woodrow Wilson was its governor. That long line of ministers and professional men on both sides of the family had been deeply marked by their Calvinist inheritance. Edmund Wilson, Jr., identified with that heritage, of which he was a nonbelieving continuator.

Jews and Judaism have a long and various history, intermixed during the Diaspora with most of the peo- ples of the world, but Wilson's philo-Semitism was se- lective, even among Jewish intellectuals. He respected

Trilling and encouraged Kazin. On the other hand, he was always slightly snobbish about Philip Rahv, William Phillips, and *Partisan Review*, which in the '30s he sometimes referred to as "Partisansky Review." Neither did he often write on the Jewish authors discovered by *PR*, such as Saul Bellow, Bernard Malamud, and Delmore Schwartz. He was interested in kinds of Jewishness that connected with his understanding of his Calvinist inheritance. For example, there is no evidence of his having been much interested in the Eastern European culture of *Yiddishkeit*, the New York immigrant variant of which Irving Howe studied in *World of Our Fathers*. In his essay on S. Y. Agnon, Wilson refers in passing to the "Yiddish humorists." But it is ancient Jewish writing in Hebrew that he mainly cared about, not modern writing in Hebrew or Yiddish. Nor did he make a special study of Sephardic Jewry. Most important, Wilson had almost nothing to say about the Holocaust, and when he did declare himself on the topic, he could seem chillingly detached. Alfred Kazin wrote me (July 21, 1995) that Wilson once remarked to him during World War II that it was useless for the Jews to try to fight Hitler, since so many of them "had already been exterminated."

We see, then, that much of what Jews consider Jewish is not dreamt of in Wilson's philosophy. What then does he honor? The answer is: everything that has points of contact with his post-Protestant commitment, especially that which may be derived from the Old Testament. Wilson's idea of the Jews is continuous with that of his Puritan forebears. For example, he responded powerfully to the people of modern-day Israel, seeing them, rather romantically, as in the same mold as the Hebrews of the Bible. Thus the appeal to him of Yigael Yadin, an archaeologist who did major work on the Dead Sea Scrolls and was later his nation's military chief of staff. One corollary of Wilson's attraction to the epical biblical Jew is that he was not much amused by the figure, so common in Jewish-American writing, of the *pintele yid*, the "little Jew." An exception is his pleasure in the comedy sketches of Elaine May and Mike Nichols. Another exception is Agnon, who wrote about the lost world of the *shtetl*, in which the *schlemiel* was a familiar type. More typical is Wilson's famous "Dissenting Opinion on Kafka" of 1947. To Wilson, Kafka was too intent on being defeated to be the great writer of the modern age; Wilson thought him "unfortifying." But he took to Agnon, whose fiction had the warmth and human interest and reflected the faith that Kafka quite lacked. His way of praising Agnon is to link him to the Bible—he declares himself ready to accept Agnon as a "true representative of that great line of Jewish writers that begins with the authors of Genesis."

Genesis marks the beginning of the Bible and also of Wilson's significant relationship with Judaism and the Jews. His superb essay "On First Reading Genesis" (1954) echoes in its title Keats's poem "On First Looking into Chapman's Homer." Both essay and poem are about the excitements of language. But whereas Keats had read Homer in Chapman's Elizabethan English, Wilson believed that no one really knows Genesis who has not read it in the original. From the very first sentence, his emphasis is on the Hebrew language: "I discovered a few years ago, in going through the attic of my mother's house, an old Hebrew Bible that had belonged to my grandfather, a Presbyterian minister, as well as a Hebrew dictionary and a Hebrew grammar." In 1952, well before he had thought of going to Israel to report on the Dead Sea Scrolls, he was studying Hebrew at the Princeton Theological Seminary, where a century earlier his paternal grandfather, Thaddeus Wilson, had matriculated before becoming a Presbyterian minister.

His most interesting observations on reading Genesis concern the lack of conventional verb tenses in Hebrew. He compares the Hebrew time sense with that in Russian, another language he had taught himself, and concludes that what has allowed the Jews to survive is their "sense of persistent values." The language itself conveys the "dimension of eternity." Wilson also discovers "the perdurable" in the characters of the Hebrew alphabet, which have "the look of having been once cut in stone." His fascination with even the mass and shape of Hebrew characters links him to the Jewish Kabbalists, with whom he otherwise has little in common. Altogether, his unqualified enthusiasm makes it possible to understand how his Anglo-Jewish friend Isaiah Berlin can have remembered Wilson as taking "more interest. . . in Hebrew [than] anyone I have ever known who was not himself a Jew."

Wilson is not the first instance of a Protestant scholar's coming to a greater appreciation of the Jews through a fascination with their language. The Israeli historian David S. Katz has written of the Jews' return to England in 1655. England's Jews had been expelled by King Edward I in 1290 and were readmitted during the Puritan protectorate of Oliver Cromwell. Katz writes that sympathy for actual, living Jews grew out of the Reformation-inspired zeal to read the Word of God in the language in which His Book had been written: "Christians after the Reformation were left alone with the Word, and in order to understand it without priestly intermediaries they were forced to arm themselves with the proper tools, including a basic knowledge of Hebrew. As was the case everywhere that Hebrew studies flourished, Christian interest in the Old Testament inevitably created a climate of theological opinion which attracted Jews, converted or otherwise." It wasn't only that Jews were needed to gain philological competence in dealing with the biblical text. It was believed by some Christian scholars that "God created the universe by speaking Hebrew: 'Let there be light,' He said, and suddenly all of existence came into being." It was thought that Hebrew held within itself the secrets of the cosmos, and thus the Jews held the keys to unlock these mysteries. I don't wish to suggest that Wilson himself entertained any such mystical conceptions of language—no one is likely to confuse him with his near contemporary, Walter Benjamin. Neither do I attribute to Wilson a religious belief he clearly didn't have, as a skeptic about all religions. But what may appear idiosyncratic in Wilson's ideas of the Jews and Judaism appears much less strange when we understand it in the context of Calvinism's high valuation of the Old Testament and its emphasis on the importance of Hebrew in studying God's Word.

It will be obvious, then, that in arguing for Wilson's self-conscious affiliation with his New England Puritan ancestors, I am not saying that he sympathized with their theology or their supernaturalism. Indeed, it has seemed to me at times that one reason Wilson praised the Jews as much as he did was his defiant identification with a people who refused, as he did, to accept Jesus as the Messiah. Jason Epstein had his doubts about the relation of Wilson's idea of the Jews to reality, doubts Wilson recorded in his journals of *The Sixties*: "Jason out of tune and grumbling, thought I overrated the Jews, on account of the New England identification with them; [in Jason's view] they were really awful people." Many Jews have expressed themselves as Epstein does about other Jews, as have blacks about other blacks, and so on. More important for my present purpose than Epstein's "grumble" is his seeing that Wilson's idea of the Jews was romantic and literary, though we ought to add that it was much more realistic than that of Cromwell's British contemporaries, most of whom had never met a real-life Jew.

One is aware, on reading what he has to say about Israelis, both in his book on the Dead Sea Scrolls and in his travel writing, that he was always looking at this country through the lens of his reading, not only of the Bible but of everything else he could find about ancient Jewish history. The scholar James Sanders believes that Wilson's careful reading of Pliny, Philo, and Josephus about the ancient Essenes still "commands

respect as a general account of the topic." What he responds to in the Israelis is their heroic fealty to the
past. According to Wilson, they refer everything they
do to events that happened on the same terrain four
thousand years before. He is clear-eyed enough to see
that at times this confusion of present and past has negative implications. Thus Wilson registers his disap-
proval of a certain Israeli "moral fanaticism" and "nar-
rowness" that have their origins in the Bible. Apropos
the Israelis' treatment of the Palestinian Arabs, he
notes "signs of returning to the callous intolerance of
the Israelites in relation to the people they dispos-
sessed." Sometimes, however, he is himself as indifferent to the suffering of the Arabs as any modern-day Israeli settler on the West Bank.

Nothing in Wilson's background disposed him to
concern for the Arabs. It was the Israelis he admired,
and curiously—in view of his own militant atheism—
he admired them most for their faith. "It is the faith
that keeps Israel going and that has allowed her to take
all these problems on, the faith of the Jewish prophets
from Moses to Aaron David Gordon [an important early
Zionist who argued the dignity of manual labor], and
the loyalty of contemporary Israelis to this." It should
be kept in mind in reading such an endorsement (for
Wilson, uncharacteristically warm) that he was responding to the Israel of 1955, when the state was only
seven years old and still animated by the idealism of
the pioneering Zionist generations. Yet Wilson appears
to be seeing what he wants to see: a people who are
able to turn the wilderness into fit habitation because of

an idea in their hearts. He contrasts the Israeli fresh-
ness with "European discouragement and cultural
staleness, the running down and falling apart."

Wilson's response to Israel incorporates his own ego
ideal, his dream of a selfhood sufficiently strong to
carry on despite the adversity of circumstance, and it
suggests a displaced version of the old Calvinist sense
of the Jews as a witness people crucial in the fulfillment
of God's design. For many evangelical Christians, it
will only be with the conversion of the Jews in their
own land that Christian history will be completed.
There is no need to claim that Wilson subscribed to
this theology if we point out a comparable, unusual
evangelical fervor in his writing about Israel. Thus toward the end of the 1969 edition of his book on the
scrolls he writes: "This millennia-spanning mixture in
Israel of ancient and modern history makes it, in my
opinion, a place of unique interest and of heartening
inspiration. . . . to visit the modern Israel and to see
what is going on there is to feel oneself partly released
from the narrow constructions of today's and yester-
day's newspaper and to find oneself, thus rising above
the years, with their catastrophes and their comings
and goings, in touch with one of the greatest human
forces for the tenacity and authority of our race."

It is hard not to be awed by Wilson's own tenacity
and authority, his industriousness and professionalism.
No one should think that everything came easily to
him. It's clear that he was vulnerable to periodic fits of
discouragement—depression may be too strong a term,
though his distaste for writers who are not "tonic" or
"fortifying" points to a fear that an author's gloom may

be contagious. And parts of *A Piece of My Mind* and the oft-discussed introduction to *Patriotic Gore* reveal a bleak pessimism that was the other side of the affirmation of the spirit in Wilson's writings about Israel and the Jews. Many of his writer friends from the '20s had not fulfilled their promise, instead fizzling out or dying young. He was determined to stay the course, and in later years repeatedly looked to Jewish history and his own ancestral tradition in reminding himself of the importance of moral courage and strength, of dedication and endurance. He had a plaque placed over the oxygen tank in his bedroom-study that said: "Be strong." This watchword, the longer version of which appears on his tombstone—"Be strong and of good courage"— was that of the early rabbis, who invoked it when they had completed one book of the Pentateuch and were summoning their resources to begin the next.

Wilson's sympathy with the Jews was imperfect in that he preferred an idealization—the modern Jew as intellectual hero, following on the Old Testament Jew as hero of faith—to the Jewish actualities all about him. Still, he showed himself to be more truly cosmopolitan than his American precursors, men like James Russell Lowell, Barrett Wendell, John Jay Chapman, and Henry Adams, all of whom knew the great world outside of New England but could never fully emancipate themselves from the anti-Semitic stereotypes of their class. The chapter called "The Jews" in *A Piece of My Mind* shows he was quite aware that his own consistent philo-Semitism marked a break with the American tradition of the upper-class WASP as man of letters to which he belonged. In a recent interview,

Saul Bellow recalls Max Weber's idea that "the Jews are aristocratic pariahs, pariahs with a patrician streak." Whether or not that self-consciousness is endemic among Jews, it showed itself at times in Wilson. It won't do to overstate his conception of himself as a pariah, inasmuch as he thought himself to be the rightful heir to an American cultural legacy. But in identifying, during the '30s, with the artist-outsider and with the Jew as champion of oppressed groups and radical new ideas, he located himself outside the existing class system. Still, he remained an upper-class radical. He liked his Communists and Jews best when they acted like spiritual aristocrats.

The central theme of the American gentleman-intellectual, beginning with James Fenimore Cooper, is the decline of the Republic. Wilson's career offers the familiar spectacle of the old-stock American of cultivation and goodwill lamenting the manifold changes that have brought his world close to dissolution. The question for such patrician intellectuals—Cooper, Holmes, Henry Adams, Robert Lowell—is how to respond to that decline. It's easier to see now than it was in Wilson's own time that, for all the jeremiads of his last decades, he came to terms with the loss of the WASPs' exclusive dominance better than most. We need only think of the anti-Semitism of twentieth-century writers of comparable ancestry like Edith Wharton, T. S. Eliot, and Ezra Pound to appreciate his uniqueness in identifying with the Jews rather than blaming them for the changes that had brought about the loss of his class's primacy. It's not simply that, unlike Pound and Eliot, he was able to resist the impulse to load onto the Jews responsibility for everything he hated about modern life. Much more than that, he positively affirmed a bond with the Jews. But what kind of alliance was it that included in its embrace an Englishman like Isaiah Berlin, an Israeli like David Flusser, a number of American literary critics, and book publishers Jason Epstein and Roger Straus?

Whatever its content or aims, it was an alliance that continued beyond his death. He designated Edel as general editor of his papers, which included his private journals. Daniel Aaron also helped to keep Wilson's work before the public with his excellent introduction to Wilson's *Letters on Literature and Politics: 1912–1972*, edited by his wife Elena and published in 1977. That his posthumous literary life was largely entrusted to Jewish scholars confirms the trend. It's true that, in absolute numbers, Jews probably made up only a small percentage of Wilson's regular readers. It's also true that his most vocal admirers have included writers and critics who are not Jewish, like John Updike and Lewis Dabney. But if we ask who has most effectively carried on his central work as a literary critic and historian, the answer would include the aforementioned Jewish scholars, as well as others like Irving Howe. The philosopher John Dewey inspired a similar loyalty among a different group of Jews who were more concerned than the tribe of Wilson with social policy issues. The allegiance to Dewey of his disciple Sidney Hook, in the '30s and after, is paralleled by Alfred Kazin's continuing attachment to Wilson over more than half a century. Both Wilson and Dewey were unchurched, liberal-minded WASP intellectuals who were thought by

second-generation Jewish-Americans to be worthy of
the considerable idealism they brought to their study of
American literature and society. Wilson, like Dewey,
figured as more than one thinker among many, seeming to his younger Jewish admirers and imitators to
stand for America itself.

It becomes harder and harder to remember that
there was once a time when writers dreamed of swal-
lowing America whole. That ambition, evident in the
young Kazin, was by no means limited to Jews, but it
was more conspicuous among writers who were to
some degree outsiders—such as Theodore Dreiser—
than among writers who felt themselves to be America's rightful heirs. The crucial decade in the history of
these intellectuals is still the '30s, when most belonged
to the radical opposition. The Depression had the effect of discrediting the Protestant cultural establishment as well as the existing economic order. Many of
the writers and intellectuals waiting in the wings for
their turn were Jewish. By the '50s these men and
women of letters had themselves become something of
an establishment, and found themselves supervising
the cultural tradition rather than trying to subvert it. It
may be that they had never been quite as alienated as
they thought, for once American society acted more
hospitably toward them, they were ready not to be outsiders. They can be accused of opportunism, but from
the start the Jews were more open to acculturation than
any other group in the great wave of immigration from
southern and eastern Europe. They eagerly learned
basic American values as children in big-city public
schools and libraries and settlement houses, all staffed

by teachers and social workers ready to inculcate "Americanism" in these most willing pupils.

The WASP-Jewish alliance has been above all an alliance of like-minded Americans in the culture-and-society tradition of Arnold. Marginalized WASP intellectuals like Wilson might more easily find supporters among culture-hungry, assimilating Jews than in the world of Gentile country clubs and corporate boardrooms. Wilson could enjoy drinking with old Princeton classmates, but except for the most eccentric and independent-minded, these would have been men who had made their peace with the new America as he never did. And however much Jewish intellectuals retreated from their earlier radicalism during the years of the cold war, they never gave in to the boosterism of the group Wilson wrote off collectively as "bond salesmen."

Since the '60s, we have entered a third stage of immigration, and the label of multiculturalism is used to reject most of the Western heritage in the name of the equality of non-European peoples of color. Meanwhile, many Jews have become part of the American establishment—at the moment, the presidents of most of the Ivy League universities are Jews, or, as in the case of Harvard's president, Neil Rudenstine, partly Jewish. And here is the irony. As professors and administrators, these Jews, now obliged to exercise power, must deal with new minorities which resist them, having a very different idea of their own relation to the majority culture. Nowadays most Jewish scholars are vocal supporters of the white, Western culture that only sixty or seventy years ago inclined to treat them as pariahs. In that distant time, identification with Edmund Wilson became one way Jewish insurgents, raised in a culture that was in truth centuries distant from the European world in which their immigrant parents had grown up, made Western humanism in American terms. Having enjoyed for less than a half century the pleasure of taking their place in the tradition which Wilson symbolized, they find themselves in the strange (to them) position of being resented as part of a white, male, Euro-American establishment.

Success in America is a complex fate, and one of its names is failure. Jewish intellectuals may still have something to learn from Wilson. They can learn an idiom once thought to be the exclusive property of the WASPs, the idiom of the culturally disinherited upper-class American.

WILSON THE MAN

A READING OF THE

JOURNALS

NEALE REINITZ

EDMUND WILSON's published journals—from *The Twenties* to *The Sixties*—are his message to the world about his life and work, a substitute for the major autobiographical novel he often contemplated but never wrote. In his journals he could speak freely about his inner thoughts, his reading, his writing, his friendships, and his sexual adventures. Instead of being protected by the supposed guise of fiction, he would be insulated by posthumous publication: as he grew older, it became clear to him that the journals should be published after he was dead.

Through much of his career, Wilson wrote novels, short stories, and plays (like *I Thought of Daisy* and *The Little Blue Light*) with quasi-autobiographical characters. But his notes and his notebooks show evidence of more ambitious plans that he did not carry out. At an early stage, he made a series of notes headed "myself imagined as a character"—a character who, like Wilson, grows up "in the early nineteen-hundreds,"

feels oppressed by the rich, suffers a nervous breakdown, and regains his confidence after the stock market
crash, when he returns to old friends and old values.
Wilson recognized, in the '30s, that the enterprise of
writing *To the Finland Station* would take him "far
afield of what I thought was my prime objective: a work
of fiction made out of the materials that I had been
compiling. . . ." Still, by 1939 he had not given up: in
that year he drew up a prospectus for a panoramic
novel to have been called *The Story of the Three
Wishes*. He planned to divide his personal experiences
among three characters—a stockbroker, a Russian bu-
reaucrat, and a bohemian writer—but when he under-
took the first part of the novel in the early '40s, he replaced the stockbroker with an aspiring composer who
shared some of his own acquaintances and appetites
but few of his intellectual interests.

It was Wilson's immersion in the past during the
'50s—which were also his biological fifties and early
sixties—which turned him away from an autobiographical novel to consider his journals in their own right.
In those years he spent summers in the eighteenth-
century stone house he inherited at Talcottville, New
York. With historical curiosity, he studied the house
and the family that had lived in it. In the same vein,
he looked into his personal past and began to edit his
journals, with the aim of preserving their content but
supplying the perspective of intervening years. He
focused his first efforts on the notebooks of the '20s,
changing, omitting, and adding passages until he came
up with the rounded and polished book, *The Twenties*.
Time ran out before he could apply the same process

to other decades. Before he died in 1972, he managed
to make some revisions in the second volume, but it fell
to Leon Edel, his designated editor, to assemble and
annotate *The Thirties*, as well as *The Forties* and *The
Fifties*. These journals were, in general, edited skill-
fully, with useful introductions. Both Edel and Lewis
Dabney, who edited *The Sixties* at Roger Straus's request, concerned themselves with issues I am raising in
this essay. The five books appeared over a period of
eighteen years, from 1975 to 1993, attractively produced by Farrar, Straus in uniform octavo editions, a
shape which invoked their author's own stubby but
stalwart physique.

The five volumes should be considered as a whole.
Wilson's European-born widow, Elena, believed that
taken together with his letters (which she edited) they
made up *"une oeuvre,"* a single cohesive work that
should be published seriatim with as little delay as possible. The protagonist at its center is Edmund Wilson,
who describes at length where he is, what he sees,
whom he talks to, what he drinks, what he reads, how
he feels, what is going on in the world outside, and
what he does in bed. The result is a work that has narrative interest, character development, and historical
setting, though it is not consistent in tone or quality.
The Wilson character changes from decade to decade,
as one might expect. But the treatment changes, too.
Some volumes are less novelistic than others, largely
because of the vicissitudes of Wilson's life, which af-
fected how often and how well he kept notes.

The reader of the journals can perceive the matrix of
Wilson's published writing growing out of his life and

character. On a simple level, his journals contain his personal responses to writers who were the subjects of his criticism—O'Neill, Fitzgerald, Hemingway, and Dos Passos, for example. On another level, they include Wilson's ideas and plans for articles, books of criticism, plays, and novels—consummated and unconsummated. More substantively, they are loaded with notes and extended "draughts" (Wilson's spelling) for his published pieces. These emerge in his journals long after the finished products appeared: the reader who knows Wilson's description of the Soviet Union in *Red, Black, Blond and Olive* can see something of how it was put together by going back to his notes in *The Thirties*. This is a reversal of Wilson's usual process, in which articles and reviews were republished in revised and enlarged form. Here the clock is set back to the origins.

Despite Wilson's insistence that he did not want to "cut any corners," the five printed journals are not simply transcriptions of the notebooks in the Beinecke Library at Yale. In these school copybooks, generally of about one hundred pages each, covering periods of time from five months to several years, Wilson wrote, in pen or pencil, notes from day to day or week to week. On the last pages and the inside covers of most of these notebooks he jotted down notes that were out of chronological order: the ideas for articles and books; lyrics of popular songs ("When my sweetie walks down the street"); odd personal names ("Bloodgood Hoskins"); colloquial expressions ("Am I burnin' yuh up?"); headlines ("Congressional Debate on Prohibition"); advertising signs and slogans ("Good to the Last Drop!"). (This material often appears in his printed journals, where it resembles the "Newsreels" of Dos Passos's *USA*.) At times Wilson simply wrote on yellow legal sheets, which he later slipped into the notebooks. He also kept notes on little scraps of paper or the backs of envelopes or letters: some of these notes can be dated by the address or letter on the front. In some notebooks there are significant chronological gaps, when Wilson was disturbed, deeply engaged in a writing project, or simply falling behind in his note taking.

The process of converting these notebooks into published journals, begun by Wilson during his lifetime, itself turned into a kind of epistolary novel, featuring Wilson's editor, his widow, and, less frequently, the scholar Daniel Aaron and the publishers Robert Giroux and Roger Straus. Until her death in 1979, Elena Wilson (who was Wilson's literary executor) offered Edel a stream of comments and corrections. She indicated what outmoded prejudices, embarrassing identifications, and sexual details might be omitted; she also reminded Edel of the correct accents in French words and details of Wilson's appearance ("Edmund's eyes were very dark brown—nearly black"), work habits ("Edmund just about never wrote when drunk"), and critical opinions ("Edmund did not like Nancy Milford's book on Zelda one bit"). Edel accepted most of Elena's suggestions, but the relationship between them was strained. He particularly objected to her desire to publish Wilson's letters in one volume for the general reader, arguing that a two-volume scholarly edition would be better and reminding Elena that she was interrupting the sequence of the journals, which she valued so highly. He abandoned his resistance as she persisted in her "homage to Edmund of everything I know about him and that was best in him." Elena received moral support and editorial help from Wilson's friend Aaron, who might have preferred an annotated edition. Aaron's introduction to the *Letters on Literature and Politics, 1912–1972* (1977) is keyed in to the literary, intellectual emphasis of the collection, which differs from the journals in its deliberate scanting (through Elena's selection and ellipses) of Wilson's intimate side.

The Twenties (1975), the volume in which Wilson's hand is clearly evident, reads very much like a novel. Wilson recommended *A Prelude*, which was published five years before his death, as a prerequisite. This unforced compilation of early diaries and thoughtful retrospective comments on family, friends, Princeton, and World War I brings Wilson up to the first page of *The Twenties*. A young man, not long out of the army, finds his way through the literary circles of the city, transcends his innocence for marriage, love, and sex (surprising some readers who had by 1975 forgotten *Memoirs of Hecate County*), and discovers that he is destined to be a critic rather than a poet, playwright, or novelist. He observes his surroundings in Manhattan: "the sky above the bulk of office buildings was high piled with silver light"; Washington Square, after April rain, is "freshened with tender green and swimming in milky pallors." But his primary business is people—his dissolute friends Ted Paramore, Scott Fitzgerald, E. E. Cummings, Dorothy Parker, and the many women whom he loved or made love to. Like another young diarist-novelist who had entered the literary circles of a great city seeking a vocation—the Boswell of the *London Journal* of 1762–63—Wilson paid the price for his adventures with a case of gonorrhea.

In *The Twenties* Wilson endows himself with a second sight that Boswell was denied. As Wilson edited the typescripts in the '50s, he trimmed his posthumous sails. He changed the names of his lovers and would-be lovers—Léonie Adams ("Winifred"), Magda Johann ("Katze"), and above all Frances, the Ukrainian-American waitress from Brooklyn (he tried "Milly," but she became "Anna," the name he had used for her in *Hecate County*). He softened the upper-class WASP vocabulary of his early years—remarks about Jews, for example, which he soon regretted. Most important, he added a great deal to the contents of the notebooks, until much of *The Twenties* became a conversation between a younger and an older Edmund Wilson, thirty years apart in age. Wilson also added to the story by filling in sections that were crucial to his narrative. He closed the gap of 1920–21, when he was too overcome by his passion for Edna Millay to write; and he supplied an account of his mental breakdown of 1929, which had been induced by a sense of failure in his love affairs and his writing. The older Wilson explains how he began to recover from his breakdown when he readdressed himself to a crucial passage in *Axel's Castle*. The younger Wilson moves on to recognize that criticism, not poetry, is to be his career: he subsequently describes a visit to the country house of Louise Bogan which inspired the title poem of *Poets, Farewell!*, the sometimes comforting, sometimes ironic, collection which brought him up to the present.

In *The Twenties* the elder Wilson comments upon other writing he was doing at that time. He explains how in 1924 he had hoped to have Charlie Chaplin perform in his ballet *Cronkhite's Clocks* (which was printed but never staged), a vivid enactment of the frenetic, mechanized office life of New York. The younger Wilson sets down an idea for "*Theater*, etc." ("The dinner guests enter single-file and in dress-suits to the sound of the stiff beats of a dirge") and a sample of a monologue to be called *The Man in the Troll Hill*. Nothing came of those. The raw materials of fiction that he had published many years before also turn up in his entries. There are scenes from *I Thought of Daisy* (1929)—parties, an attempted suicide, the concluding day at Coney Island. Looking back, the elder Wilson says of the chorus girl Florence O'Neill: she was "the original of Daisy in the novel, but the story itself is invented—we were never lovers." *The Twenties* contains long introspective passages that had been uttered almost word for word by the would-be satirist who narrates *I Thought of Daisy*: "Literature is merely the result of our rude collisions with reality, whose repercussions, when we have withdrawn into the shelter of ourself, we try to explain, justify, harmonize, spin into an orderly pattern in the smooth resuming current of a thought which for a moment has been shattered and torn by them. . . ." Wilson's notes on a drunken visit to Boston four days before the execution of Sacco and Vanzetti show how he had adapted the flippancy of this jaunt into the insidiously satiric irony of his short story "The Men from Rumpelmayer's," published in 1927. Wilson also printed in *The Twenties* an assortment of rather ragged unpublished poems, after warning the reader to "skip any verse he sees coming." Most of these pieces are addressed to Edna Millay ("the winter stars I gave her / She has long since spent for cigarettes").

The Twenties ends with Wilson's respectful farewell to his first wife, Mary Blair, of whom little has been seen; *The Thirties* (1980) begins with an idyll three months later with his new wife, Margaret Canby. The contrast between the two volumes is great: the Wilson of the '20s becomes the Wilson of the Depression. The novelist and poet turned critic is soon absorbed in politics, labor strife, and everyday life. Out of the visits to factories in Detroit, scenes of mining strikes in Kentucky, Hull House in Chicago, and Washington at the height of the New Deal—all clustered in this volume—had come the articles written for the *New Republic*, ultimately collected in *The American Earthquake*. Wilson included in the text of the journal his declaration in the summer of 1932 that he would vote for William Z. Foster, the Communist candidate. His extensive impromptu notes on his 1935 visit to the Soviet Union are much livelier. This was a trip, paid for by a Guggenheim fellowship, to broaden his background for *To the Finland Station*, which was already appearing in the *New Republic* in serial form; the notes provided the basis for the Russian section of *Travels in Two Democracies* (later enlarged in *Red, Black, Blond and Olive*). Eight pages of *The Thirties* are given to Wilson's notes for *Beppo and Beth*, a play about a sophisticated couple living the high life in the face of the Depression. He finished the play and published it a few years later, although he was unable to persuade the Group Theater to produce it.

The counterpoint to Wilson's preoccupation with politics and economics in *The Thirties* is an emotional life as romantic and sensual as his experiences of the '20s, one which entered his published writing only in *Memoirs of Hecate County*. At first, his marriage to Margaret Canby resolves the guilt and conflicts that had played a part in his breakdown described at the end of *The Twenties*. But her sudden death in an accident in September 1932 evokes a long, intimate, at times remorseful recollection of their life together. In the remaining journals, even into *The Sixties*, Wilson records dreams of Margaret, in which she is still alive but not quite attainable. She had provided the model for a major character in *The Higher Jazz*, his then unpublished offshoot of *The Story of the Three Wishes*, and a minor character in *Hecate County*. After her death, Wilson's notebooks from 1934 to 1937 describe erotic encounters with Louise Connor and Elizabeth Waugh, both disguised in his code—an initial one letter earlier in the alphabet: Louise is "K." and Elizabeth is "D." (Elizabeth had become the Princess with the Golden Hair in *Hecate County*.) The interludes with Frances, as "Anna," were minimized in *The Thirties*, a point of agreement between Edel and Elena. (Edel said that "her presence takes the reader back too much to *The Twenties*.")

Wilson's editor and his widow also agreed that *The Thirties* was "much more of a book" than *The Twenties*." Edel thought it was "the 'big' volume of the journals, having a very particular kind of historical unity."

Indeed, here Wilson is at least in the wings of the historical drama, while in *The Twenties* he is in the audience, making a few remarks about Hoover and Lindbergh. In *The Thirties* he undergoes myriad adventures in industrial and political heartlands at home and abroad, talks to political leaders, suffers the loss of Margaret, and returns to his amours and friendships. But there is no sense that his character is evolving while all this goes on. The events come to no resolution. There is a letdown after the Russian journey: the volume ends on a minor key in Chicago and Cape Cod, where Wilson is living with Mary McCarthy, whom he had married in 1938. Unlike *The Twenties*, *The Thirties* does not demand that the reader stay close to the progress of the hero; instead, it offers the opportunity to venture at will into the surrounding world. The question remains whether Wilson, had he lived long enough, could have effectively provided a denouement of self-discovery. *To the Finland Station* was a culmination to his '30s, as *Axel's Castle* had been for the '20s, but the impact of outside events may have frustrated an attempt to show continuity in the inner life of the journal keeper.

Wilson's inner life appears only sporadically in *The Forties* (1983), the slimmest of his journals, chiefly of interest as an exhibition of his workshop. (Elena noticed this imbalance, and commented on it shortly before her death.) Wilson became the book reviewer for the *New Yorker*, and reported on his trip to England, Italy, and Greece, shabby and depleted in the aftermath of a war of which he had disapproved. The notes for these articles and subsequent visits to the Zuñi

Indians in New Mexico and to Haiti bulk large in *The Forties* and afford comparison with their final versions in *Europe Without Baedeker* and *Red, Black, Blond and Olive*. Edel nourished the volume by printing, in rather careless fashion, Wilson's outlines and notes from 1939 to 1942 for *The Story of the Three Wishes*. The editing of *The Forties* is not up to the standards of Edel's diligent approach to *The Twenties* (to which he supplied an introduction) and *The Thirties*; there are numerous errors, including what appears to be inadvertent repetition of passages from *The Thirties*.

In this decade of distractions, the thread of Wilson's personal feelings and reflections is taken up only toward the end. In the early '40s there is very little on his dysfunctional marriage to Mary McCarthy; one erotic passage that she vetoed for publication remains among his papers at the Beinecke. Wilson's character comes to life in his sensual and aesthetic pleasure at his marriage to Elena in 1946. He records his delight in sexual details to which Elena, who had read the manuscript, made no objection. In 1947 he responds to the tragic death of Katy Dos Passos in an automobile accident. In 1948 he writes a moving account of a visit to the aging, trembling Edna Millay two years before her death, notes which formed the core of his tribute to her in the epilogue to *The Shores of Light*.

The Fifties (1986) celebrates Wilson's return to the house in Talcottville. He becomes involved with his cousins, his neighbors, and his friends, and is pleased to identify himself with his great-grandfather Thomas Baker, who had acquired the house for his mother's family. Wilson first wrote about the house in 1933, at a time when he was busy with more compelling issues, in "The Old Stone House," an article marked by an acute sense of history. He planned but did not complete a play about it in the 1950s; and in "The Author at Sixty," an essay in *A Piece of My Mind* (1956), he took stock of his life at the age at which his father had died and declared his summer residence in Talcottville. In the journal of *The Fifties* Wilson's reacquaintance with the house and his personal response, important events in his life, are chronicled in detail. Unfortunately, he had anticipated himself by including the entries on Talcottville in *Upstate*, an account of twenty summers, published in 1971, the year before he died. *Upstate* was one of Wilson's most popular books; in it he weaves the Talcottville details into a continuous narrative supplemented by family and regional history. This leaves for the reader of *The Fifties* who already knows *Upstate* little more than an opportunity to compare the texts. For the earlier published version Wilson had removed some personal passages, such as the details of his quarrels with Elena; she hated the stone house and seldom went there, preferring to remain at Wellfleet, Cape Cod, in the house that Wilson had bought in 1941.

Lengthy notes for *Apologies to the Iroquois* are barely integrated into the text of *The Fifties*. The most interesting pages of this volume—a section which is mainly new and is central to Wilson's life at this time— describe his rediscovery of Europe on a grand tour of 1954 and a shorter trip of 1956. (He also visits Israel for his studies for *The Dead Sea Scrolls*.) He immerses himself in the cultural world of England and France, recovered from the desolation of 1945. He talks to writ-

ers and critics in Oxford and London and he discusses
literature with the octogenarian Max Beerbohm in
Italy. He spends some time with Elena's disoriented
aristocratic family in Germany. Despite his continuing
defensiveness, especially toward the English, Wilson
comes to recognize that his "determination to make
something out of America must have biased me against
what was really good in Europe." But except in special
circumstances, he still believes, an American "has no
business here."

A conspicuous shortcoming in *The Fifties* is the absence of any contemplation of the direct literary effects
of Wilson's establishment as country squire and citizen
of the world. He gives no sign that his personal history
is as interesting a literary subject as his family history.
In fact, he began assembling collections of his articles
of the '20s and '30s: the literary *Shores of Light* and the
"documentary" *American Earthquake*. Most important,
he was finally making the decision that he would tell
the story of his life and times in his published journals,
not in an autobiographical novel. In *The Fifties* Wilson
says nothing of beginning to edit *The Twenties*—although it meant, in effect, that he was working on two
volumes of the journal at the same time.

Wilson was now committed to the journals as a literary testament, but he knew, at sixty-five, that he would
not have a chance to reshape his current notebooks.
The first paragraph of *The Sixties* (1993) sets the bal-
ance between acceptance and persistence that runs
through this volume: "*Jan. 1, 1960. At my age*, I find
that I alternate between spells of fatigue and indifference when I am almost ready to give up the struggle,

and spells of expanding ambition, when I feel that I can do more than ever before." During a long period in 1960–61 he made no entries while he was finishing *Patriotic Gore*; at other times in *The Sixties* he attempted to fill in the gaps in note taking, more often than in earlier volumes. What emerges from these efforts is a book of nine hundred pages—by far the longest of the journals—that is driven by the experience and imagination of a man who is reaching the end of his life but lives it to the full as long as his strength holds out. Wilson's swiftly moving account is a virtual novel, more somber, yet more expansive, than *The Twenties*.

The reviewers of *The Sixties* have overemphasized the presence of decline, pessimism, and death. The dark shadows seldom cross Wilson's mind during the first part of his narrative. Indeed, they gradually lengthen through the book, but even then they cannot obscure the curiosity and intellectual vigor of his day-to-day notes. In the early years, Wilson is secure in his vocation and can indulge his enthusiasms for Auden and Stravinsky, Mike Nichols and Elaine May, and pass verdicts on Malraux, Hemingway, and Tolstoy. He is now a distinguished figure on the world stage, and beyond his three bases of Talcottville, Manhattan, and Wellfleet enjoys friends, exchanges ideas, and observes the culture of Toronto, London, Paris, Rome, Budapest, Israel, and the White House. He evokes the past in short but poignant flashes (of his former wives, as well as Edna Millay and Frances) and revisits scenes from World War I. The Talcottville sections of *The Sixties* are an integral part of the texture of Wilson's life, not the addenda they seem in *The Fifties*; they include

a greater number of revelations that were omitted from
Upstate. Apart from a few poems, no other "draughts"
are included in *The Sixties*, although Wilson refers
from time to time to the many articles and books he is
writing and revising. He is engaged in disputes with
the U.S. government (over income tax), with Nabokov
(over the translation of *Eugene Onegin*), and with the
MLA (over the American Authors' editions).

As Wilson nears seventy, his fatigue and indifference
increase: observations on the uselessness of life and the
pointlessness of sex become more noticeable. He records in 1964, at sixty-nine, "[a] feeling, the older I
get—which I never expected to have—that earthly
matters are hardly worth the effort." This is an echo of
the more energetic angst of 1927, when he attacked the
"dignified and pompous" ways in which philosophers
try to cover up "the ludicrous puerile inadequacy of the
only accounts one can give of the conditions of our existence." At seventy, he writes in two quatrains that "My
body, stiff with ailments, stalks a cage / Of rooms; my
mind, though ranging, loses speed, / Now entering the
dark defile of age." He chronicles a daily routine which
grows more arduous, with uncomfortable nights, sleep
induced by Nembutal and whisky. After a remarkably
active trip to Jordan and Israel in 1967, on the eve of
the Six-Day War, with a stopover in Paris, his strength
begins to ebb, although he is working on the Dead Sea
Scrolls, reading Balzac, and entertaining Svetlana,
Stalin's daughter, at Wellfleet. In his seventy-sixth
year, as his sexual powers and physical health palpably
fade, he clutches at sensuality with two barely disguised younger admirers, enjoying the perquisites of a

literary celebrity. The entries become fewer in Wilson's last year. He refuses a pacemaker, but he is still writing, still reading. He evidently wrote the last entry in the Old Stone House on June 11, 1972, the day before he died.

Wilson has it both ways in the five-volume oeuvre of the journals; without writing an autobiographical novel, he achieves the purpose of one—an author's perspective on his own life and work. One might summarize the plot, as if for Masterplots: the aspiring novelist recovers from a breakdown to write a pioneering study of modernism and make his place as a critic; in the '30s he is swept up in politics, endures personal tragedy, visits Russia, and writes a history of Marxism; later on, as a critic for the *New Yorker*, he returns to his ancestral home and his biblical roots; in old age, as his powers leave him, he faces death with equanimity, as if he is accepting—with resentment—an unpleasant fact. Of course the narrative quality is uneven: only *The Twenties* and *The Sixties*—his entrance into the life of a critic and his leaving it—enjoy the unity and concreteness of fiction. The middle books need only be read selectively, according to the inclination of the reader. Each volume, in its way, yields an insight into the relation of the man to his writing.

Wilson made a wise decision in not trying to construct a novel. Had he tried to show his development in this way, he would have been driven by his ideas into an unwieldy theoretical framework, as he was in *I Thought of Daisy*. He uses the narrative and descriptive powers which might have made him a novelist, finessing the inability to distance himself from his subject, which make much of his fiction talky and intellectualized. What emerges is a self-portrait of Wilson that does not conform to any of the clichés that have been applied to him. The enormous variety of his writing has made it difficult for his critics to get his character into focus; they have chosen to see only the Wilson they want to see: the curmudgeon of "Edmund Wilson regrets," his all-purpose repsonse card; the sensualist; the man of letters; the political activist; or the "public intellectual" (the current favorite). To the readers of these journals he is, as he wished to be seen, all of these things: an irascible, argumentative, loving, insatiably curious Everyman. The man who denounced World War II and the cold war, who read Genesis in Hebrew, and who played sexual games in his mid-seventies with his dentist's wife, is the man who, on the last page of *The Sixties*, remembers a line of Tennyson's Arthurian poem *Elaine* and (without identifying the source) cites Swinburne on a painter's praise of "the wonderful breadth of beauty and the perfect force of truth in a single verse" of Tennyson's poem.

THE PERSPECTIVE OF

BIOGRAPHY: 1929,

A TURNING POINT

LEWIS M. DABNEY

[Wilson had spent the fall of 1928 in a beach house in Santa Barbara near that of Margaret Canby, who would become his second wife. Separated though not yet divorced from Mary Blair, he had found sexual satisfaction with his mistress of the preceding year and a half, Frances Menihan, to whom he was more deeply drawn than he could acknowledge. He was on leave from the *New Republic* revising *I Thought of Daisy*, his first novel, and pulling together the materials for *Axel's Castle*.]

THE YEAR 1929, which was to prove as significant for Wilson's private and emotional life as for his work, began with a series of shocks. He came back to New York before Christmas 1928, having heard just before he left that Elinor Wylie had died December 19. Only forty-three, she'd fallen that summer and had a stroke at the home of a British country squire for whom, unbeknownst to the critic, she was suffering from unre-

quited passion. Wilson and she had spent less time together after her marriage to William Rose Benet, yet
she had written to him ebulliently of her love for life
and poetry. Wylie's was the first death among his close
literary friends, and the memoir he published six weeks
later in the *New Republic* ends with its author bereft in
a darkened world. In Santa Barbara he'd received a
wire that Herbert Croly had also been victim to a
stroke. When he got back to New York, his partially
paralyzed boss discussed the future of the magazine,
confiding that Bruce Bliven (then managing editor, not
editor, as Bliven recounts it) was not an acceptable successor, an opinion Wilson shared. His salary was raised,
and Malcolm Cowley believed that Croly was groom-
ing Wilson to succeed him. Within a year the editor
would be dead and become the subject of another impassioned memoir, even as Wilson started going on the
road as a reporter, moving the magazine to the left with
his first reports on his country in the Depression.

In the first days of 1929 he prepared to send *I
Thought of Daisy* off to Scribner's, unsure what he had
accomplished with all the revision. He sent a copy to
Edna Millay, hoping she wouldn't be offended by the
portrait of the poet Rita. Instead, she offered to rewrite
Rita's speeches, finding Wilson's dialogue inferior to
his analysis, and he awaited her suggestions. A four-
page interpolation in the journal mentions the "letdown" he sometimes felt after finishing a book, and recalls how, as winter gripped the city, he retreated to
his "narrow, stale-smelling" room on West Thirteenth
Street to write the introductory chapter of *Axel's Castle*. He was incorporating Whitehead's *Science and the*

Modern World and his memory of Gauss's lectures on nineteenth-century French literature to work up the background of modern poetry.

Frances came occasionally to see him, but they were uncomfortable in the squalid room and, as he cryptically observes, "it was difficult for her then"—she surely guessed he had spent the three months away with another woman. From California Margaret reported on a lunch with Ted Paramore, who, she said, approved of her and Wilson as a couple. She also announced plans to open a hat shop in partnership with a friend, a venture she hoped would pay for her next trip to New York. When the couple were at a literary gathering not many months afterward, one woman believed Margaret was merely ducking intellectual conversation when she declared, "I'm interested in hats!" Conscientiously, she kept up with the current books and encouraged Wilson's work, and her letters are loyal, yearning—"Goodby my dear," she writes on her new "Margot" stationery. "Bear me in mind as I do you, constantly—especially at the hours between 4–6 A.M. as I have developed a habit of wakefulness at this time." They got along well and she very much wanted to marry him; yet to the critic, mulling things over on Thirteenth Street, it seemed that "we did not have enough in common."

He also heard from Léonie Adams, with her regrets at having "moped and quarreled" on the day she sailed for France. Her entertaining commentary on the literary scene was evidence that she felt "more myself than I have in a long time." In London, she recounted that "H. D. has been having me to teas with half-mad people, and the chief personage in her own household is a night-blooming monkey with owl's eyes, which they have to lock up to prevent his biting them while they sleep. I am next being taken to see Dorothy Richardson, whose husband does up his hair in pins. The only really sane literary person I have encountered is Mr. Robert Trevelyan, who passes about petitions against capital punishment at tea." A trenchant report followed on her Paris encounter with Gertrude Stein: "She had written a command: You will come, quite simply—and she said she is a pure California product. She even gave a resume of American literature bringing it down from Emerson to herself as the consummate flower of American genius. That is, for abstraction and pure intellect." Displaying the mind and wit that had drawn Wilson to her before their ill-advised sexual encounter, Léonie adds, "It may be all right as regards Emerson, James, and Stein, but she put in Mark Twain, Whitman, Poe, and in fact every considerable figure, in the abstractionist hierarchy. With poor [Ford Madox] Ford a yard away she pointed out how he had absorbed and misapplied James, as Joyce had herself, since in their low European way they are caught by experience."

Wilson was to pay a price for the previous spring's excesses. Feeling some unnameable "obstruction" against Margaret's plans, but afraid to fall into the same demoralizing indecision he had had about how to serve in World War I, he wrote to Léonie that Margaret and he were thinking of getting married. The affronted young poet shot back a furious claim that he had made her pregnant. Implying she'd had a miscarriage, though rather confusedly mentioning a "torn membrane" that was "healed" by a London doctor in October, she excoriated his "fiendish" behavior. Later the same day Léonie sent another letter, apologizing for having "worried" him, wishing him happiness and adding that he had helped her to become a better person. She then wired to the *New Republic*, warning him not to tell Allen Tate "about it" (the pregnancy). He evidently replied that he despised himself, for on February 15 she wrote, "You mustn't hate yourself on my account," explaining how much she'd wanted a child. She'd had a miscarriage "about August," of which she was unaware till she saw the doctor in London. To Wilson's suggestion that there were better men than he for her to marry, she replied that she believed him "on the whole the best person I have known," concluding she had grown up emotionally by learning to accept her absolute aloneness and "the hostility that must underlie every human contact."

Wilson was not in New York to receive her third letter, for guilt, along with his irresolution about Margaret and his heavy drinking, led to a nervous collapse. The draft of the first chapter of *Axel's Castle* breaks off, and in his interpolation in *The Twenties* he writes: "I found that I couldn't sit down in the evening and work at my book in that ghastly little room, and I took to drinking and going alone to Noel Coward's current revue, which would appear to me at the time amusing but, when I was sober, come to seem disgusting, as the silly little tunes ran through my head. *Teach me to dance as Grandma did* has always been associated in my mind with the nauseating smell of my room."

Liquor had become integral to his routine and he absorbed quantities at night, yet after the sedative effect wore off, emerged in the morning with no visible signs of a hangover, eager for the working day. Now, however, the alcohol triggered anxieties:

At last, when I set out, at the end of one week, to go down, as usual, to Red Bank [where his five-year-old daughter Rosalind was living with his mother], I found myself seized with panic as soon as I got into the taxi. The symptoms were a good deal more serious than they had been on my visit to Princeton, at the time of my anxiety about the war: I began to tremble violently, and I realized that I could not go down to my mother's. I called up Aunt Caroline and asked her to recommend a doctor. She sent me to a young G.P. who simply thought I had been drinking too much and had me spend a couple of days in the hospital, putting me to sleep with a dose of morphine.

The diagnosis was plausible if Mary Blair was right that he was consuming ethyl alcohol, the cheapest, crudest liquor available. But when he got out "the symptoms returned" and he feared he "was going insane," having always "had a fear of this kind, on account of Father and Sandy." The previous fall, before leaving for California, he'd paid a grim visit to the sanitorium to see his cousin. Sandy's fate had settled upon him after almost a decade of institutionalization: "face at last profoundly changed: thinner, harder, grayer, more mature and more staring." In that room looking onto a "green slope, beyond the barred windows, all golden-green in the late afternoon sun," Sandy had stated flatly, "Life's all right if you can stand it."

Alarmed by his seeming inertia and malaise, Wilson telephoned John M. McKinney at the Neurological Institute in upper Manhattan, and the Freudian psychiatrist received him late that night at home, appearing in his bathrobe. Reassuring him he "was not going insane," McKinney pointed out that he was almost thirty-five, his father's age when the senior Edmund's morbid hypochondria had begun, and explained, "Neurotics are strong people. It's like polarization in physics. The neurosis is the other side of a positive assertion of will." This matched Wilson's observation of both his father and Edna St. Vincent Millay, and the "nerve doctor," as he terms him, kept him functioning at a time when, as he would later tell Rosalind, he sometimes "thought there was a pencil writing for him all by itself." He remembered these weeks as the worst of his life, for "the panics and depressions continued" until "it seemed to me I was condemned, by some power I could not control, to destroy myself in some violent way." At this point McKinney persuaded him to go to the Clifton Springs sanatorium west of Syracuse, which pioneered by treating alcoholism and neurasthenia without drawing a clear distinction between them. Drinkers and nonviolent mental patients were housed in the same ward, a fact that instead of threatening Wilson the doctor must have known would make it clear he was not crazy. But "it was the dreariest point of the winter, and the bleakest part of northern New York," he recalls.

"The spell I spent waiting in a reception room that has a plain wooden clock on the wall was something I cannot describe."

That wooden clock remains on the wall of the old hospital, now a rest home, where in 1929 arriving patients got off the Lehigh Railroad's Black Diamond from New York, which made a special stop, and signed themselves in for a minimum of a month. Wilson found the clinic and its routine "boring beyond description," yet he felt secure there. Put on a drug called paraldehyde, he liked its "exhilarating relaxing effect," believing he conned the elderly night nurse into giving him more by reading poetry to her. Mr. Irving Hubbard, who retired as chief pharmacist after being at Clifton Springs since World War II, explains that they undoubtedly wanted him to consume as much as he would, since the point was to wean him from alcohol and an addiction to paraldehyde could be broken— among other things, the drug made one continually flatulent. He struck up an acquaintanceship with an elderly artist, and Mary Blair sent a cheery letter, reporting that their daughter, at the moment visiting Pittsburgh, was getting on well with grandmother Blair and attending school with cousins. Mary offered him her apartment for a few days after his release, saying she'd move to a hotel. Writing at a table amidst the other patients in the stark, high-ceilinged room, Wilson resumed *Axel's Castle*. So thoroughly was his sense of rational control invested in the critical role that he knew he was recovering when he was able to revise "the passage in which I tried to explain symbolism." He sent *Daisy* off to Max Perkins, thereby missing Edna's rephrasing of Rita's speeches and other improvements which she had belatedly addressed to New York. He put finishing touches on and typed up his accumulated poems for the collection *Poets, Farewell!* and wrote to ask Gauss if he might dedicate to him the "book on modern literature."

In Mr. Hubbard's experience no one got out of Clifton Springs in less than a month, but after three weeks, Wilson recalls, "I finally insisted on leaving in spite of their reluctance to release me." The therapists undoubtedly feared he would begin drinking again— Mr. Hubbard adds that some of the alcoholics had booze so effectively integrated into their working lives that they could never give it up, people whom the attendants, not entirely facetiously, called "the geniuses." Back in the city and at the *New Republic*, Wilson for a time continued with the paraldehyde, but McKinney, he says, warned him not to drink too much of it, a convenient excuse to go back to alcohol, this time for life. The doctor also tried to help him overcome his neuroses. When recommending psychoanalysis to a friend in 1937, Wilson spoke of having been "psyched," and Mary Blair would report McKinney telling her that her husband had "a mother complex." To Rosalind, however, Wilson said, "He wanted to get me on the couch," and in *The Twenties* he declares, "I hate the sense of dependence" and thus "detached myself." Like other writers of his generation, he did not necessarily want relief from the "wound" that was somehow a part of his talent. But in the first years after his breakdown, as *The Twenties* notes, he suffered a "sense of floating in a void outside the world of other human beings, where one's ties are not felt as binding, the dreadful feeling of not being real, of not being a part of society through either purpose or relationship, the strain of associating with people combined with the fear of being alone." It was some time before he "recovered from what I suppose were manic-depressive 'mood swings': moments of liveliness or heartiness would be followed by a despondency and silence that people did not understand and that made me, I am afraid, at the time, a rather uncomfortable companion." He could at last empathize with his father's gloomy self-absorption. At the senior Edmund's death it had been enough to blame the Gilded Age, but in "When All the Young Were Dying," written in New York in the late spring of 1929, experience enables Wilson to plumb the misery marked by the felt-lined bedroom door:

> Now I, more arrogant in a wiser day,
> But half my life behind me, son of that father,
> Know what blind life, what tomb of solitude,
> What doubt, what draining of the spirit's blood,
> Were ended where you lay.

To his readjustment after Clifton Springs Léonie contributed a note of bitter comedy. When he wrote from the sanitorium, she sympathetically replied that she too had difficulty concentrating, "and it would do some kind of good to see you, although you may not understand about that now." She then wired: "I AM TOO UPSET TO WORK UNLESS YOU ARE CERTAIN YOU CAN SAY NOTHING TO MAKE ME FEEL BETTER I WILL COME TO TALK TO YOU." He was evidently certain; two weeks

later she wired him at the *New Republic*, "I AM IN A BAD
WAY AND MUST AT LEAST UNDERSTAND." Unable to toler-
ate the idea of someone suffering more than she, she
ignored his evasions, and in the journal he recalls having "to face Winifred [the name used to disguise her in
their brief sex scene], who had quickly come back from
Europe and with whom I had harrowing interviews."
He would later observe to Mary McCarthy (who, she
confided, rather wished she had this gift) "Léonie always made me feel guilty." It was an effect she had on
others: to the writer Judith Farr, Adams' former student, she was "a beautiful spirit," who could make you
"feel guiltier than anyone else could ever do. You always felt you hadn't done enough, hadn't tried enough,
hadn't understood enough." Wilson's torment was
ended by Léonie's confidante, Louise Bogan, now married to his classmate Raymond Holden, a minor poet to
whom he deemed her as intellectually superior as he
did Elinor Wylie to Benet. More experienced, since
she'd married first at nineteen and had a child, Louise
eventually advised him Léonie's pregnancy had been
imaginary. In a new burst of angry letters Léonie accused them both of betraying her, yet her intellectual
friendship with Wilson soon reasserted itself, and when
he persuaded her that they had not made fun of her for
her confusion, she reconciled with Louise. One can
trace the result of Bogan's act of mercy—which he
would reciprocate during her breakdowns of the early
'30s—in his account of a visit to her Hudson Valley
farm early in July. A journal passage describes the lush
countryside, picturing the misty valley at nightfall, the
hills and the long summer grass, the sun setting and the

moon clear with its pure colors in the sky above, the far lake, the headlights on the distant road. Swimming in a deep quarry, with its "warm gusts and icy veins of springs," the relieved writer envisions "against the white lights of the setting sun, the bodies of the bathers, like spirits drawn by Blake, outlined in the light, as if half-transparent and radiant themselves."

Though Wilson recalls making up his mind to marry Margaret after returning from Clifton Springs, he in fact remained uncertain what to do as his relationship with Frances deepened. "Though I tried to conceal my collapses, she always knew at once what was happening, and this made me feel a little better, for it meant that my solitary experience, my frightening isolation, was being understood, and hence shared, by another human being." Their lovemaking is more intensely registered in the journal. "She was lying at the foot of the bed—I at the head," he writes in a passage which John Updike has cited appreciatively. "I saw her eyes over her hips—soft-hard and round—like cunning burrs—burrs like agate marbles—with their unexpected depth, especially when the rest of her face was hidden." Frances resumed chronicling her impoverished and harsh but vital milieu, opening up to him—as he would say of "Anna" in "The Princess with the Golden Hair" fifteen years later—"that new Europe of the East Side and Brooklyn for which there was provided no guidebook." Meanwhile he was writing to Santa Barbara. In January Margaret relished the thought of his "beaming face," but she picked up on the tension in his letters, wishing she could "embezzle the shop's funds and jump on the train," and was distressed when he brought her up to date from Clifton Springs, hoping he wouldn't "get tied up in knots again my dear." She urged him to go ahead with the divorce from Mary and accepted his suggestion that they find small apartments across the corridor from each other in New York the next January. At last in June, able to share a compartment on the train with a wealthy friend, she came east and spent two weeks with him, including a day at Coney Island. But no mention of her visit appears in the journal, and the moment Margaret leaves, Frances and he are passionately reunited. "I still loved her so I kissed her till her mouth was bruised," he notes. Frances defines love as he does—"I love it, being made love to! I could be made love to forever!" A week later, she models for him the new red dress he has bought her. With a freedom of feeling seldom found in the early journals, he writes, "Her nose was all swollen from my whiskers kissing her—her hair, which was almost smooth, only slightly waved, smelled clean of tar soap."

The vacillation of the narrator in the *Hecate County* story and his inner struggle against finally losing "Anna" thus go back to 1929, though the character of Imogen derives from a later phase of Wilson's life, after Margaret's death. From Santa Barbara Margaret expressed regret that he wasn't to spend another fall with her and offered "to come and valet [him]" that winter, asking where he expected to be living. The end of August found him again happily in Frances's arms. A parenthesis in the journal speaks of a fictional character with an impulse to strangle the woman whom he is "more and more determined to marry." Only a few days later, however—as Margaret's happy reply indicates—he urged her to come on at once and committed himself to proceeding with the divorce. The journal suggests the reason. On September 5 or 6, after mentioning the abortions she and a friend had once obtained for thirty-five dollars, Frances kidded him that she might be about to get pregnant: "I think I'm swelling up down there—I don't know whether it's because I eat a lot and have been drinking a lot. . . [laughing] I'm worried!—I'm gonna be sick and I don't think I'll see you any more all week." Perhaps testing the waters, she said, "Funny to have a little Edmund running around the house." Wilson's first biographer concludes, without supporting evidence, that she was pregnant and "aborted Wilson's child in September 1929." But would he have wanted Margaret, from whom he had hidden the affair, to rush East for the occasion? It is more likely that Frances's teasing—perhaps after missing her period, or a day or two of it—scared him into action. In Pittsburgh in 1923 he had observed the grim preparations for the abortion Mary and he had not gone through with. Given the equally distressing prospects of fathering a child and of putting Frances in the hands of a back-alley hack, he decided to end their relationship.

Margaret tried to heed the summons. Twitting him for his impulsiveness ("You must admit you are sudden—after not hearing from you for about a month you present a scheme which would barely give me time to buy a ticket"), she made plans to let her house, arranged to leave Jimmy with his father for the year, and broke the news to Miggs, her business partner. Knowing that to go through divorce court with Mary would be hard on him, she wrote, "Just take a drink and you won't mind." Yet she found it difficult to leave California. Jimmy's father had lost most of his money in the crash, which threatened the custody arrangements, and her mother begged her to stay on till Christmas. It was almost enough for her that Wilson wanted her back. Reminded of "the many times I stumbled across the sand at five A.M. returning from your house," and seeing "everything the same," she wrote, "I am looking forward so to being with you again that the spark of life in me is being nursed along by the knowledge." Ironically, on the day she was invoking these romantic memories, Wilson lost his resolve and persuaded Frances to spend the night. The next morning the sight of the "capable young woman, in her green dress, ironing her apron on the card table" evoked "a memory of sweetness and dearness—affection, satisfaction." Though Margaret was presumably soon on her way, he once more asked Frances to move in, an offer she declined, saying it wouldn't be right for her daughter Adele. In November he left the Cummings's flat on Charles Street for a small place on Ninth Street. The thought of Frances settled cozily in his own apartment, lounging around in his spare pajamas, was almost too much for him. Two years after his life had been changed by their becoming lovers, he was still surprised to find she cared for him, noting that, in a moment of worry about her family, "she put her arms around me and kissed me as if I meant something to her—as if to embrace me and be embraced brought some relief."

He documented on separate sheets instead of within the journal what he believed were their last weeks, twenty-odd pages interweaving stories of her life with scenes of them together. The gulf between their worlds remained—"She didn't think of writing as work—didn't think of me as working because I didn't work with my hands." Knowing they were soon to part made him silent and moody, and early in December, when Margaret wired she'd be on the train in a week, he finally told Frances the truth. "So you were thinking of marrying somebody else all the time!" she said. Confessing that she had tried to get involved with another man, she boasts in the journal page called "Last Days," "I'm going to get someone who can do it eight or nine times." She says good-bye with, "Well, I'll have to look for another lover," and warns him "not to cheat on Margaret." On Christmas Eve he found that she had given him crab lice, like the gonorrhea almost three years before, yet this malady proved convenient, since it eased his Prufrockian retreat into the bourgeois world to which Margaret's love was binding him. Looking back with a bitter realism, he notes that Frances "began to fade into the dinginess of some of my first impressions of her, to blend with and disappear in the grayness of the winter pavements." New Year's Eve he left a desultory party for the Childs franchise on Broadway where she worked and, ordering corned beef hash with a poached egg, surreptitiously "slipped her $10 in a package of cigarettes."

Through all this personal drama (with the class conflict emphasized by the opposition of Anna and Imogen in *Hecate County*) the critic did some of his most important work of the decade. On the page he could summon a clarity of vision and purpose he lacked in personal relations. Sometimes—as when writing the journal notes that are halfway between Hobbes and deconstruction—he doubted whether "the sober judgment which, by an effort, I was sometimes able to muster in print" was worth "the disappointments and humiliations of a life which never hit the mark or suited the means to the end." Whatever the effort involved, his writing before and just after his collapse at the end of January is masterfully grounded and sensible. "I begin to wonder whether the time hasn't arrived for the intellectuals, etc., to identify themselves a little more with the general life of the country," he suggests to Tate when posting checks for the poet's *New Republic* reviews. In a review of the diary of Dostoyevsky's wife, written after he returned from Clifton Springs, he asserts that, like the "nineteenth-century Russians," American writers needed "both to adapt European culture to the alien conditions of American life and to cultivate from our own peculiar and un-European resources an original culture of our own." "Dos Passos and the Social Revolution" and "T. S. Eliot and the Church of England" followed in April. Where Dos envisioned a sturdy army of workers eschewing the temptation of new cars and radios in order to build socialism, Eliot preferred a world of highly literate seventeenth-century churchmen, and Pound "a medieval Provence where poor but accomplished troubadours enjoy the favors of noble ladies." Mencken—who had once seemed so bracingly American—took society as "a sort of German university town, where people drink a great deal of beer and devour a great many books, and where they respect the local nobility." Urging writers not to be fooled by their imported myths, imaginatively useful as these might be, he thought that Americans had to make sense of their world because it was quickly becoming "everybody's world."

He was getting on with *Axel's Castle*. The introduction to the modern writers he had finished at Clifton Springs appeared in the *New Republic* at the end of March, and the chapters on Yeats, Valéry, and Eliot that fall, with the Joyce coming in December. The intensity of his absorption in the task is suggested by the editor Robert Linscott's anecdote of Wilson talking about *Remembrance of Things Past*. One night when Linscott had been invited to dinner, "as Edmund was raising the first spoon [of soup] to his mouth, I asked him a question about Proust," whereupon he "lowered the spoon and started to talk. Now and then he would pause, lift his spoon, then under pressure of another thought, lower his spoon and continue his talk." Through the next courses of fish and dessert, brought in by an old servant, "he was all the time raising and lowering his spoon but never getting it to his mouth." As Linscott finished the meal, Wilson appeared to be "coming down to earth," and finally glancing at his guest's place, he exclaimed, "Why Bob, she hasn't given you anything to eat." This is the background of his extraordinary paraphrase of the eight-volume novel, which had persuaded him he could make the moderns more accessible, as he subsequently wrote to Perkins from Santa Barbara. Yet his reservations about their "resignationism" and "discouragement of the will" were real, and his breakdown sharpened his ambivalence toward Proust, who in the cork-lined chamber too much recalled Wilson Sr. behind the felt-lined door. When revising the book a year after the Crash, the revelation of reading Marx would help him tie this chapter together by taking Proust's world as the dying capitalist one.

As though with an intuition that the whole ground of American culture was about to shift, in the last group of lyrics for *Poets, Farewell!*, written in the summer of 1929, he bade farewell both to youth and to the "nonsense and inspiration, reckless idealism and childish irresponsibility" of the '20s. The pastoral verses headed "Hillsdale" after Bogan's country home link their fading to that of three-and-a-half centuries of English lyric poetry:

We have rhymed under gray skies in the stubble
    grass—
Sped plunging motor-rides with drunken song—
Had Wyatt with breakfast, Yeats with the final glass,

"I leave that speech to you who have the tongue," he concludes, a concession to all those (Stevens, Frost, Pound, and Pound, among them) whose imperfections he had proclaimed a few years before. Two sonnets characterize Millay and Bishop without naming them: Edna is seen pursuing fresh experiences as if with "sleepless demons" on her track, while John remains

baffled in exile—"the very language of that vision lies,"
Wilson declares of their exuberant defiance in *The Un-
dertaker's Garland*.

His final poem followed an August weekend with the
Cummingses at Silver Lake in New Hampshire. Ann
Barton, Cummings's rakish second wife, who had earlier that year sent Wilson a telegram inviting him to
make love to her (LITTLE BIRDIE OUT OF THE WEST WILL
YOU FLY IN TO MY LOVE NEST APRIL 15 WOULD BE BEST
RSVP), encouraged him to bring a woman along, but he
declined. He enjoyed long talks with the poet, and reported to Tate that Cummings was shrewd about the
world yet interested only in the gifted individual, the
artist. He was "the pure romantic," a type that might
not survive much longer, "though perhaps I think this
merely because the romantic in myself has recently
been giving up the ghost." Returning home on the
State of Maine Express and looking out the window at
a "molten lake of cold and silvered lead," he imagined
that before the landscape's spell was broken,

> I shall have plunged and weighed
> Dark waters with my stroke—
>
> I shall stare round and see
> That black receding brink—
> Let breath and arms rise free
> And all the body sink.

The metaphor of physical death suggests the release of
a former persona. As of yet, he has no clear alternative
to project into the future.

Events were to provide one. He had been troubled by the bitter textile workers' strike dragging on that summer in Gastonia, North Carolina, and in mid-September 1929, Ella May Wiggins, a young widow active in the Communist-organized union, was killed in a conflict between an armed mob and the strikers. The *New Republic* had not sent down a reporter—Dos Passos, who wanted the assignment, had been judged too far to the left, and T. S. Matthews, in Asheville for a wedding, was asked to stop by Gastonia, where he reported that nothing in particular was going on. The episode renewed Wilson's sense that the liberals were falling down on their responsibilities, as in his savage parody of his own partying the weekend before the executions of Sacco and Vanzetti, "The Men from Rumplemayer's." The beginning of the collapse of capitalism on Black Tuesday took him by surprise. He had declared that writers should be realistic about their society, yet had not (as he looked back on it twenty years afterward) "exercised enough insight to realize that American 'prosperity' was an inflation that was due to burst." A secularized Protestant, Wilson had once described in a droll movie review desert prophets inveighing against Mammon and "the gigantic finger of God" writing out "its warning on Belshazzar's wall," and the Crash, for him, was "almost like a rendering of the earth in preparation for the Day of Judgment." Literature did not always satisfy his need for belief, and in the midst of the economic and social crisis the Marxist faith, of which that May Dos had appeared naively credulous, would seem rational and progressive. It

justified his dislike of the broker's world ("One couldn't
help being exhilarated at the sudden unexpected collapse of that stupid gigantic fraud") and promised a
more equitable system. The respect for ordinary humanity which a year as an army private had created—
and to which Frances's character and her stories had
given new depth—now made him grow to detest the
smugness of the privileged when "ordinary people"
were eating out of garbage cans.

The Twenties ends with Margaret's arrival and
Wilson's divorce from Mary Blair. He did Mary a favor
that summer, helping her to pay for a trip to France, for
she had wanted to see Paris and believed she might
work out some theatrical connection there. Her letters
show her trying to enjoy herself, though put off by the
cost, bored both by tourism (Paris for her, she found,
was just a Coney Island "without the roller coaster")
and by her fellow Americans, especially Margaret
Bishop, who "talked about her house—her servants—
her furniture—her new pajamas—her new bathing suit
and whatnot." Mary hoped that her daughter might
someday see Paris, and she worried about Rosalind.
After sailing back from London, she made her last efforts on stage, writing from Wilmington, Detroit, and
Chicago of her usual disappointments with the play or
the company. She had discovered that actors could be
tiresome conversationalists—"They sure do live, sleep,
and eat personalities." She urged Wilson to stop drinking, as she claimed to have done, taking him to task
when she phoned one evening and he was tight. In a
letter from Chicago she seems once again the witty
Mary Blair who had been such fun to be with after

Edna Millay left for Europe. "You can imagine how hard up I've gotten when I buy a *New Republic* and read your articles. You must have done a lot of work on the T. S. Eliot one. I thought it was very good." Consulting a lawyer about the settlement, she hopes "we can get things fixed up all right so it won't be too long till you can have some new foundation."

She filed a charge of adultery, and they were divorced February 3, 1930, the decree, according to form, forbidding Wilson's remarriage except with the judge's permission. Mary showed up at court drunk and weepy, but they parted on friendly terms. "When I finally left her in her apartment, after dinner, she gave me a human intelligent look, as she said good night, which made me feel her friendliness and her strength—a look of understanding between us on a level away above our wrangling—I could count on her, she counted on me," he writes in the final paragraph of *The Twenties*. Briefly she would try again to hold onto him, irritated at not seeing him in connection with Rosalind, urging him to bring Margaret to visit her. Several months after Wilson remarried, however, she would do the same.

Margaret's train arrived December 21. Having written that she hoped his troubles were about over and they ought to "get drunk together" to celebrate, she came straight to his apartment, later checking in at the Brevoort. Perhaps this was the time she dropped one of the clever lines that are attributed to her in the journal—"I busted my boiler to come east for you." They spent two wintry January weeks at a country inn in Riverton, Connecticut, getting the critic out of the city on

the anniversary of his breakdown the year before. To
Bishop he wrote, "I've come up here to get away from
New York and do some work," and he set about
confidently surveying the intellectual scene, from the
dogmatism of Irving Babbitt and Paul Elmer More to
the need for a political alternative on the left, the limitations of a Marxist reading of American conditions.
The couple took brisk walks in a landscape whose
majesty didn't ease Wilson's sense of isolation: "Here
am I among elms again," he notes, that "pillar the clear
night, strong as the heavenly vault," with the nearby
river "always falling at the door." The experience
yielded a poem, completed three or four years later, in
which his life is sublimated in an art intended to resist
time, as do the stream and the elms "dark on white
dwellings, rooted among rock." He echoes Pater's gem-
like flame. "They flicker now who frightfully did burn
/ And I must tell their beauty while I live," Wilson declares of the fading energies of friends like Fitzgerald
and Millay, anticipating his own role as memoirist and
curator of reputations:

> Changing their grace as water in its flight,
> And gone like water; give me then the art,
> Firm as night-frozen ice found silver-bright,
> That holds the splendor though the days depart.

In the journal, this scene contains but one passing
mention of Margaret. Though their early months of
marriage would be deeply satisfying to both, by the
time he published the poem "Riverton" she would be
dead—a victim of alcohol as well as, on another level,

the burgeoning social commitment toward which her husband turned his energies and passion.

He would one day tell Mary McCarthy that she was "living a novel when she should have been writing one." In 1929 he had lived a tale he could not write except in the disjointed fragments of the notebooks, poems, and criticism, here pieced out with the help of other people's memories and the letters of Margaret, Frances, Léonie, and Mary Blair (he destroyed his letters to Margaret after her death, and those to Mary were destroyed by her sister, while those of Frances and Léonie have been lost). It is a story Wilson himself would never understand except in the most general of metaphors, much as Fitzgerald interpreted the movement from the '20s into the Depression personally, paralleling the nation's financial collapse and failure of morale to his own. He was more fortunate than Scott insofar as the confusion of his life somehow fed the order of his writing. But in both life and work he had summed up the decade and put it behind him, and the terror of his breakdown, in a measure, prepared him for the coming crisis of society.

The journal contains a more convincing welcome to the end of youth than he had achieved in fiction and verse: "When all our ideas of honor and loyalty, derived from our social class, from our Renaissance education, from our foolish early fantasies of ourselves, have been broken up and carried off by the currents in which we find ourselves drowning, we are at a loss what to fall back on, but we are bound to fall back on something; and this is perhaps where the real conscious solidarity

of the human race begins," Wilson writes. The codes of
his background would, in fact, be with him for the rest
of his life, but honor and loyalty had meant little to
someone drowning in a belated sexual fulfillment and
all its human complications. From the convergence between his individual experience and that of the culture
arose that sense of "the real conscious solidarity of the
human race" which drives the quest for justice in his
reporting during the Depression years. He overcame
the extraordinary inner divisions of 1929 when he
could integrate the writing and acting of history in his
celebration of strength and revolutionary will, *To the
Finland Station*.

REMEMBERING
EDMUND WILSON

ELIZABETH HARDWICK,
JASON EPSTEIN, MARY MEIGS,
ROGER STRAUS, AND
ALFRED KAZIN

THE FOLLOWING are reminiscences exchanged at the Mercantile Library in the spring of 1995. Hardwick, Epstein, Meigs, and Straus spoke in a roundtable moderated by the editor, Meigs, largely reading from her autobiography, *Lily Briscoe: A Self-Portrait*. Kazin's talk was given on another evening. Most of what was already known to readers of his books has been omitted here.

Elizabeth Hardwick: I don't feel I knew Edmund Wilson very well, though I knew his work and keep going back to it. I only saw him at Jason Epstein's, and a few times at Wellfleet, as well as several times in my own house in Boston. But I remember moments of embarrassment. It was his way with people to think they could tell him something, but of course, you often couldn't. And when he was working on *Patriotic Gore*, he somehow got the impression that I wasn't entirely a Northerner, and so kept asking me about the Civil War. At that time, I didn't know very much, I wasn't really sure that there were two battles of Manassas or Bull Run, or just what Pickett's charge was. But Wilson would go ahead and talk on the subject, and that was really a rare, most unusual experience. He did not lecture; quite the contrary, it was all movement and enthusiasm and knowledge. Even if he was chattering away about, say, the Bible, which he knew a good deal about, it was just like gossip, really. It was that offhand.

On one occasion, in Boston, I wished that I had not invited a person who was keeping a journal, because I was afraid he would write the evening up in great detail. Robert Frost was there, and it had been said and was thought that Edmund didn't like Robert Frost very much. He didn't like this person who was running around and giving all those lectures and all those readings to big audiences. However, that evening he met the real Frost, who was enchanting and original, and of course changed his mind.

The same thing happened with T. S. Eliot, whom he had doubts about. He thought here was someone too cold and too royalist and too, I don't know, conservative isn't quite the right word, but too Episcopalian, too Christian. When he found out that Eliot had married a younger woman, and when the news got around that not only had they married but they sat around holding hands and sort of cuddling and being very affectionate in public, and sometimes in quite an embarrassing way—that really made Edmund think, well Eliot's all right after all. And also he found that both Eliot and his new bride, Valerie, were very much a match for him in the martini ring. So that went well.

Anyway, one more thing I wanted to report, maybe I read it someplace, maybe someone told me, but I do think I heard him say about learning Hungarian at an advanced age, that impossible language—I think it was in your house, Jason, that he said he felt like one of those old men in Balzac, huffing and puffing to his last liaison.

Jason Epstein: In the last fifteen years of his life, the years when I knew him and saw him frequently, Edmund had pretty much given up on the American government, and probably on America as a nation. The anarchic streak that had been there all along and had turned him, when he was a young man, against Woodrow Wilson's war and later, unfortunately, against FDR's war, had broadened into a river by the time of Johnson and Nixon, two presidents whose character and deeds were completely alien to his sense of humanity and his dream of America. This alienation did not prevent him from wearing a McGovern button on his necktie in the last weeks of his life, in 1972. Perhaps this was to please Elena, who was an avid member of the League of Women Voters and took voting extremely seriously. It was Wilson's alienation, however, that I suspect explains the bitter introduction to *Patriotic Gore* and the naive comments on the subject of the cold war and the income tax.

Yet, for all his despair, he never, as far as I know, lost his confidence in individual human beings, his belief in their capacity to make more of themselves and of their world and to go on learning—and teaching him. In this sense, of course, he remained deeply American. For example, he had convinced himself, completely inaccurately, that I knew Hebrew and could teach him something about it. I knew nothing about Hebrew, but whenever I saw him in those years, he would ask me whether I knew Hebrew or not. I suppose he assumed that in the interval between each occasion I'd learned it, but that's what he was like. Nor did he, even near death and with great physical suffering, ever give up on himself. He worked to the end, and, in keeping with the spirit of the '20s, kept falling in love to the end—an amazing achievement for a man racked with pain, approaching death. As you may know, in his last year or so he was involved in two active love affairs, even though he could hardly breathe.

Edmund was by nature a pedagogue. He was always in search of a promising new student. And this, I believe, is what his love affairs were really all about. He wanted all his life to learn and to teach, and this was also, I think, the basis of all his relationships, with men as well as with women, which is why he was determined that I knew Hebrew and could help him learn it. It was the essence of his literary work, learning and teaching. I was young enough to assume that this double preoccupation was not so unusual, that I would encounter it again and again in one person or another. But I never did. I have known countless writers who, with very few exceptions, wanted fame or money or revenge or immortality, or simply to impose themselves on others. But Edmund shared none of these qualities,

either as a writer or as a human being. He was utterly
selfless in his work, wanting only to learn and to teach.
In that sense he was unique.

What I myself learned from Edmund I can never
repay. I've always thought of him as my teacher, my
only teacher really. I lack those gifts that he had for
clarity, for industriousness, his gift for language, which
can never be reproduced. He will eventually prove to
be one of the greatest of our writers. Not so much for
his individual works—he had no *Moby Dick*, no *Wings
of the Dove*, no *Gatsby*—but as perhaps the greatest
teacher our literature has ever produced. I can't tell
you how much I miss him.

Mary Meigs: Edmund told me from time to time
that he was in love with me. My reaction was my usual
one of withdrawal and wariness, coupled with the
certainty that it couldn't possibly be true. Or if it were
true today, it wouldn't be tomorrow. And when
Edmund said to me "I don't know *why* I'm in love with
you," I said, or rather shouted, since he was getting
deaf, "I can't imagine." It was just as I'd thought: there
was no reason; it had nothing to do with me. I longed
to think, but did not say so, that I was like those other
women he had loved, remarkable in one way or another, but he never gave me the comfort of comparing
me with them. Did he love me not for myself but
because I didn't seem to care whether he loved me or
not? How had the others been with him, not his wives
but the others he'd loved, did *they* seem to care? Did
he kiss them, striking his solid pose like a knotty-mus-
cled acrobat about to swing someone up on his head?
Did he make love to them? Did he appreciate my

balancing act, walking the precarious wire between resistance and receptivity?

"You're really a sort of lesbian, aren't you?" He said
this to me one evening when we were alone and I was
in the state of slight apprehension I always felt with
him. Part of my ethic was to conceal my fear—of bodies, of kisses, of passion, to protect our egos (his, the
male's, and mine, the sort ofs). His definition of me
had stiffened my pride to try simultaneously not to be
prudish and not to be encouraging. But he, with his
strange intuition, seemed to know exactly how far he
could go without my fleeing. He would kiss me (I see
him now, bearing down, striking the pose) without
undue insistence, stand there heavily, or help me on
with my coat. Even in his ancestral house, with my
friend Barbara Deming in the next room, after drunk-
enly prowling the corridor, he tottered into my room in
his dressing gown and seated himself on my bed—even
there, something gentlemanly (or was it the thin
walls?) yielded to my refusal, stated calmly, loudly, to
make him hear, though I was quaking inside. Instead,
we went downstairs and talked about marriage. "What
would you like to be married to?" he asked. And I said,
"I'd make a terrible wife."

The daytime Edmund was a marvelous companion,
with his enthusiasm for everything under the sun, and
my only fear was that the awful words he sometimes
applied to others—"He or she is a bore"—might be applied to me if my responses were stupid or ignorant.
But as I look over the letters, postcards, and valentines
from him that accumulated during my years in Wellfleet, I realize better now than when I first read them

that I needn't have worried, and I'm moved by the
courtly sweetness that permeates them, as if he needed
the protective medium of the written word to express
his most delicate feelings. He had a habit of sending
small colored engravings of fish with messages on
them. I look at one of a pale blue fish resting dejectedly
on an exotic shore: "I have missed you since you left—
feel more and more like the picture on the other side,"
says Edmund. And a little poem accompanies the dol-
phin of the ancients:

> The Dolphin is extremely wise
> Turns rainbow colors when he dies;
> But when the Dolphin thinks of you,
> He turns a special, lovely hue.

He did his best to educate me, and I tried very hard
to read what he suggested. At the end of his life, he was
still wistfully writing, "I miss you." I did not dare, during all those years, to accept his friendship with the joy
it should have given me, but clung to it with secret
pride and suffered torments when he was cold, angry,
or seemingly indifferent. When he died, I was living in
France, but I felt his absence with a sense of desolation. He had enlarged my life with his myriad enthusiasms, with his programs for the improvement of my
mind, with his brutal truths. It was enlarged even by
my resistance to him and by the anxiety I felt.

> This is a Valentine note for Mary,
> of whom I am fond, and even very.
> I sometimes dream we are sitting astride
> A bicycle, taking a bicycle ride.

Edmund sent me this in 1960, one of a series of valentines we all exchanged to lighten the winter in Wellfleet. He and I dreamt about each other now and then
(I dreamt after his death that he was seated at a round
table, wearing the mask of Queen Victoria), and sometimes, we even dreamt the same dream. It was about
going into a house of old things, going from room to
room, seeing depressing changes. And then, the house
was threatened—by a superhighway, or by sinister
people surrounding it, or by crumbling walls. It was
our past, that house, what we cherished of the past—
stolen, mutilated, or decaying.

We belonged to the same generation, he had said.
We shared the ability to be moved to tears or to feel a
rush of joyful emotions in the presence of something
beautiful. Edmund read Yeats to us (when he had
begun to walk slowly, groaning, up the hill to our
house), his voice becoming unsteady at "Till the
wreck of the body," and breaking at "A bird's sleepy
cry," unable to finish. Edmund was moved to tears
by Yeats who, bare as a bleached bone at the end of
his life, still used nature for his grandest image: "Like
a long-legged fly upon the stream / His mind moves
upon silence." Edmund's mind must have moved easily
upon silence.

Roger Straus: Unlike Edmund, I am no journal
keeper. I don't think any publisher should be—probably go to jail if they did. I think of Edmund, really, in
flashes of things that happened. When Farrar, Straus
was very young, a few years old, I got a telephone call
from Robert Linscott, an editor at Random House, and
he said to me, "How would you like to publish Ed-

mund Wilson?" Obviously, I thought he was putting
me on. And so I said, "What's that all about?" And he
said, "Well, he doesn't get along with Bennet Cerf"—
who was then the highly self-publicized publisher of
Random House—"and he therefore would be free." I
said, "What can I see?" He said, "There's a manuscript," and the manuscript came over and, I guess,
that was *Classics and Commercials*. And naturally, as
soon as I saw it I wanted it, and arranged a meeting
with Edmund. And I see that first meeting, where I
couldn't have been more uneasy. In college I had read
Axel's Castle, which impressed me. I was flying blind
otherwise, but we established a strange and interesting
relationship, which I was very passionate about holding
onto. And we used to meet in various places.

We would meet at my office on lower Fifth Avenue.
We'd have lunch at Charles's restaurant, which is long
gone, and we'd talk and he would tell me what he was
working on and when he hoped to have it for me to
publish, and ask how much money was I going to give
him for it. And then we'd argue back and forth. It was
quite fun. He was his own agent and he had no editor,
really, at Farrar, Straus. He became friendly with an
editor called John Peck, who acted as a sort of copy
editor for him. And we had these strange conversations, then lunch would be over, and in those days,
down on lower Fifth Avenue, there were three or four,
if memory serve me, rare book shops, and we would
leave and he'd go cruising those bookshops, buying
this book or being given that book in a way that I admired. He was studious about the whole thing. It was
absolutely great.

Time went on, and I see another flash, much later, and much more shocking in a way. Edmund was in Wellfleet and he called me on the telephone—by this time, obviously, we knew each other reasonably well— and he said, "Roger, can you hear me, can you understand what I'm saying?" I said, "Yes"—the voice was a little thick—and he said, "I've had a stroke and I'm waiting for the ambulance to come to take me to the hospital. I want to remind you of your promise to me that you're not going to allow any of my journals to be changed when they are published." And I told him that I did remember. At the time he had finished editing *The Twenties* and was just beginning to edit *The Thirties*. And it was strange, because this was one of the few arguments that we had. I suppose I shouldn't say this, but when he was considering who was going to be in charge of his journals and his literary effects, there were two possible choices. One was Leon Edel, who was respected for the work he had done on James of course, and the other was Dan Aaron. And so he said to me, "What do you think?" I recommended Aaron, but he said he was going to choose Edel. I asked why, and he told me why, how distinguished and knowledgeable Edel was. He asked, "Why do you disagree?" I said, "Well, you know, Edmund, you're always telling me you want everything in the journals published, and I'm prepared to do that, but Edel is a bit of a prude. I'm not sure this is going to work out the way you want it to work out." And in fact, at some point later, Edel and I did have various disputations about what should go in and what should come out of the various journals.

A biography of Wilson was just published, by some-body you may have heard of, and there's nothing good to say about it except one thing. The writer—who is a typical kiss-and-tell writer, if you can dignify or undig-nify it by that—did go to the trouble of reading one book of Wilson's which I published, which was sort of fun to publish, and published because it was fun, not as serious publishing. That was his *Night Thoughts*. There were a lot of throwaway lines in *Night Thoughts*, which are absolutely—well, very personal, very deli-cious. And the other thing that Edmund did, which was incorporated into *Night Thoughts*, and which Mary Meigs has mentioned, was to write not only valentines but Christmas cards and jingles, and so forth and so on, that he would send to friends, former lovers, present lovers, and occasional enemies. And they were very, very good. I mean he wasn't exactly tilting with Robert Frost as a poet, but he did like to have his own jokes. And this biographer has used this material.

I think Wilson was a great writer. I think he was a great man. Of the various authors that I've published, he was not only the man I admired the most but the man who gave me the most pleasure to be with over a long period of time. He was lovable, and I thank my lucky stars that I was able to be his publisher for over twenty years.

Epstein: I remember the first time I met Edmund—Roger told how he did. I was a very young man and wanted to publish *To the Finland Station* in my new paperback series, the Anchor Books. So I sent him a postcard, or a letter, rather, and he replied by postcard, saying that would be fine. And we agreed on a price.

He then came down to New York on some other errand and asked me to meet him at the Princeton Club, which was then at Thirty-ninth Street and Park Avenue, an old Victorian, mahogany kind of place. And there he was sitting at the bar and I joined him, and we introduced ourselves, and he said to the bartender, "A half-dozen martinis." And they came. They were those small martinis that in those days you got in academic clubs of that sort. But even so, half a dozen, and they were all for him. I had another half-dozen.

One time in the early '60s, the first and, I think, only time I visited that extremely uncomfortable house he was devoted to in upstate New York, Edmund's mother's ancestral mansion, it was just crumbling and the town itself had become a kind of Dogpatch, overrun by juvenile delinquents, as he called them. And it must once have had a pleasant lawn in front, but subsequently the highway was built right under the porch. The cars would zip by. But he would sit on the porch in the mornings, dressed in his white linen suit and his panama hat, with his cane, like the grand seigneur of the town, and wave to people as they went by, the juvenile delinquents on their motorcycles and so forth. We drove up to the southern shore of Lake Ontario, by way of Watertown, to a place he had gone as a child to have lunch. It was a kind of Elks Club that served people in general—it was terrible. But on the way back he was full of nostalgia and began to sing the lines of a little song from the '20s in his high-pitched voice. I'll never forget it—"She's a poor little kid who don't know what she did / She's a personal friend of mine." The following day he took us out for a picnic to the Sugar

River, which he had written a lot about, it turns out, in his diaries. He was very fond of this river. And we finally came to a place where we settled down to have our picnic, but there was no river, there hadn't been a river for a long, long, time. It dried up and, I think, someone dammed it farther up. Anyway, it wasn't there at all. But he thought it was. He was strangely related to his environment, wherever it was. He would invent the environment he wanted to be in, whether it was actually there or not.

Meigs: I admired the Talcottville house—I thought it was very handsome. And it seemed to me that his attachment to it was very justified and correct. As for the Sugar River, it was something of a trickle, but it was a genuine river, and the sides of it were lined with great stones. Edmund would send Barbara and me off to hunt for fossils, and we were enchanted by the Sugar River and lugged home tons of fossils from it.

Alfred Kazin: When I was a young man, living a very typical life of a son of Russian Jewish immigrants in Brooklyn—going to City College, wondering how I could stay off relief—Edmund Wilson seemed to me everything, and I knew I wanted to be like that. I was in Provincetown part of one year, finishing *On Native Grounds*. I would gaze with fascination at the sight of Wilson on his bicycle, going to the Portuguese bakery across town. I didn't dare to speak to him; he was always, wherever he was, a subject of gossip and comedy, a figure of charm and so on. Later I realized there was more to it than that. Sitting there in Wellfleet, at Cape Cod in the wintertime, when he was editing the remains of his great friend F. Scott Fitzgerald, well it was not a cheerful place to be, in that big house, sort of a ghostly house. And it made him shiver he said sometimes, and he didn't go anywhere else. He couldn't afford to.

In 1942 I finally published my book, and, of course, a copy was sent to Wilson. You have to understand he was in a very bad way that year. He was poor and he was an isolationist. He didn't like the British or understand why we were in the war. And when *On Native Grounds* was sent to Wilson, he was married to Mary McCarthy. I went to his place in New York, and he had nothing to say about my book, which never interested him at all. But without any request on my part, McCarthy told me that it was a terrible book and would never survive. Fortunately, I didn't really take her seriously. I thought she was very pretty, but otherwise I didn't take her seriously. I never could, because at the *Partisan Review* she was famous for the fact that all the Jewish fellows who edited the magazine were afraid of this Irish girl from Seattle. But at the moment I was devastated. And I walked out, feeling very depressed, not knowing whether to tell my folks about what a failure I was.

Wilson came out with me, and he said to me, "Why don't you write about her some time?" And I thought, *oi*, what a marriage this is. We walked outside. It was raining. At that time, the elevated railroad was all over New York, including on Third Avenue. As we were standing under the tracks, I realized the kind of mind he had when he said to me, "Kazin, what do you think of the cabman's shelter scene in *Ulysses*?" I wanted to say, Mr. Wilson, the rain is falling all over me, but I was charmed. How wonderful, I thought.

Wilson took every area for his own. He knew more Hebrew than I've learned since my bar mitzvah. He knew more Russian than my parents ever knew in Russia (that was easy, they didn't know any Russian). One of the last times I saw him, he said, "Have I given you my lecture on Hungarian yet?" I said, "Not yet." He was having a bit of an affair with a Hungarian woman up in Talcottville, where Elena, his last wife and a wonderful woman, didn't like to go, and, typically enough, he was learning Hungarian. He was the most learned man I ever knew, and over the years I got to know him well, with love, exasperation, and most of all amazement, that the same man could be so wonderful in his writing and sometimes so ridiculous as a person. He would say such foolish things. He had all these conspiracy theories and, when Bobby Kennedy got shot, in 1968, he said, "Well, there's more there than appears, you know," and I said, "Oh, for god's sake, Edmund, don't go on about that; you talked that way about Oswald." And he said, to my absolute amazement, "Don't forget my legal background." He meant his father's knowledge of the law.

You must understand that Wilson had an extraordinary way of talking. People say that it arose because his mother was stone-deaf and he had great trouble reaching her. It was also because he was rather nervous around people. He didn't like to talk in public or to lecture. When he taught, he just read from his manuscripts. Wilson spoke in a sort of gasping way, in a high

voice, saying, for example, "Oh, oh, oh—Mr. Bellow."
And then he said, vaguely, "Congratulations." That's
when I realized he may never have read a line that Saul
Bellow had written.

Edmund was very much a man of his own period,
and for me he emerged from the background of the old
New Republic, where I was a hack reviewer early in the
Depression. The *New Republic* was full of young men
like myself, who were desperate for reviewing jobs. We
used to get ten or fifteen dollars for 150 words. At the
offices over on a side street in Chelsea, between the
elevated and the docks, there was something I called
the hunger bench, where we waited. To get the full effect of the lines with which Wilson ended his chapter
on Proust, you had to be poor, a radical of sorts, and
above all, amazed to find a critic who could write like
this: "Proust is perhaps the last great historian of the
loves, the society, the intelligence, the diplomacy, the
literature and art of the Heartbreak House of capitalist
culture, and the little man with the sad appealing voice,
the metaphysician's mind, the Saracen's beak, the ill-
fitting dress-shirt, the great eyes that seem to see all
about him, like the many-faceted eyes of a fly, domi-
nates the scene and plays host in the mansion where he
is not long to be master." Ah. My friend Dick Hofstadter, great historian-to-be, and I used to read this to
each other and say, "What a writer!"

Wilson was as sedately arrogant as he looked. He
once boasted to me that he had often rewritten in his
sleep the book he had just been reading. I once reviewed one of his books, *The Shores of Light*, for the
New Yorker. Wilson then wrote for the *New Yorker*

and, when he came to the office one day after lunch, no doubt full of Scotch, he saw a galley proof of my review, read it, and made a few changes in it. It was my review! Who else would even have thought of anything so awful? So typical of his arrogance. Though I loved it in certain ways, I wanted to kill him for it, too.

When Wilson did his last work for the *New Yorker*, not long before his death, George Steiner, who's a brilliant man but the most unbelievable egoist I've ever known, said, "I have replaced Edmund Wilson." And somebody said, "Oh, shut up, Steiner, you haven't replaced him. You merely succeeded him."

Wilson took ideas, especially his own, with deadly seriousness, but he was far from being an original or even a consistent thinker. His convictions were unbelievably obstinate, especially when they reflected his disillusionment with ideals he once held. After decades of working on *Patriotic Gore*, his Plutarchan history of Civil War personalities, his bitterness in the '60s about the general state of the country led him to condemn Lincoln as another Lenin. Imagine that—this got rid of two old heroes at once. The joke is that Wilson had begun the book decades before in a kind of professional Northern family that adored Lincoln and believed the Civil War was a holy war—as indeed it was.

Wilson defiantly called himself a journalist, but more so than most journalists, he was a relentlessly equipped scholar. His honesty and thoroughness at mastering a new text thrilled me. He was a teacher, a personal example, and I owe him much for showing me how to put a great writer's vision into one's consciousness. He had a particular gift, which Lewis Dabney has character-

ized, for putting the writer into a fresh historical perspective, inserting the writer with his book in some
great historical drama, such as the road to Michelet
through Marx, that ended with Lenin's arrival at the
Finland station in Petrograd in 1917. Incidentally, you
can still read *Finland Station* with enormous pleasure.
It's like reading Gibbon.

And Wilson identified with the kind of idealism
which people of that class—you have to remember that
Wilson on his mother's side was descended from the
Mathers—took from the original Puritan aristocracy. It
was a family history full of people who at one point
were utterly contemptuous of working for the big
money and of capitalism, which in our day have become so de rigueur that no one even thinks about it.
That appealed to a son of the immigrant working class,
whose parents were tortured by poverty. I hardly
needed the Depression to be suspicious of moneyed
power, or to see that in this society money is the first
measure of all things, and the final measure of many.

I don't think Wilson cared very much about race
relations. He did say to me once he thought Jimmy
Baldwin's essays were fantastically brilliant, and he was
happy and proud as a liberal about that sort of thing,
but he didn't pay much attention to what we now call
minority writing, and he was terrible about the Jews
during World War II, because he was against the war.
But he was the reverse of an anti-Semite. He loved the
way that orthodox Jews ask for more strength at the
end of the liturgical year. He was thrilled that he knew
enough Hebrew to learn these words, and every morning he would say them to himself. But he said to me

over and over again, "We must learn to live without religion." This man made a point of being the foremost atheist of an atheistic generation. All these writers who had gone through World War I had come out of Christian homes, and became great exponents of the idea— as Hemingway put it in "A Clean Well-Lighted Place"—all is nada, nada, there is nothing but nada. Wilson had the anger of a man who came out of that Christian heritage and was disillusioned. Disillusionment at the end was very strong with him—about socialism, about America, too. Yet somehow he retained his fundamental beliefs.

It was typical of Wilson that he adored Isaac Bashevis Singer's writing but most of all adored Singer's knowledge. When Wilson liked somebody, it was almost always somebody he could tap for his knowledge. One bright fall day during a taxi ride down to the old *Daily Forward* building on East Broadway, which the famous Yiddish paper was leaving, Singer said to me, "Is it really true that Wilson has those Hebrew characters on his gravestone, that he admired them so much?" Anyway, Singer said to me in the cab, "He really, he really has this on—on his gravestone?" I said, "Yes." He said to me in Yiddish, "Impossible to believe this is such a country." And I said, "Bashevis, but it is."

THE ADMIRABLE MINOTAUR
OF MONEY HILL

MICHAEL C. D. MACDONALD

LYING ON his belly in the sand with a book, his back to the sea, my father was unaware of an unusual expedition from the beach at Newcomb's Hollow: Edmund Wilson was making a rare excursion to our Phillips Beach and its backwoods bohemia. My father hadn't been in Wellfleet since the '50s, when it had become a battleground after Wilson's marriage to Mary McCarthy had acrimoniously collapsed and Father had strongly taken her side. His meetings with Edmund were usually brief ones in the corridors of the *New Yorker*. Their occasional encounters were pleasant: Wilson's diary notes meeting Dwight Macdonald at a party, the latter assuring him that he was always on his side, presumably in battles with the MLA or the IRS. Father also liked the way Wilson bypassed small talk in their chance meetings to plunge into some scholarly interest, in medias res. "I gather you're working up X," he'd begin. "Now I wonder, Dwight, what you make of his peculiar obsession with Y, and how that reflects his odd friendship with Z?" Recalling this, Dwight would smile. "No nonsense about Wilson," he'd say. "Hadn't seen him in two years, ran into him at the eighteenth-floor elevator—got right to the point! And, well, why not?"

Now, beneath a cloudless blue sky in the summer of 1971, Edmund Wilson slowly advanced up the shoreline, his tall, willowy wife Elena at her husband's side. Without telling Dwight of their approach, I ran down to greet them. Walking with a black cane topped by a gold head, Edmund was leaning on Elena's arm. He wore his usual formal beach outfit of dusty black Bermuda shorts, yellowing white shirt, and stained panama hat: "I have only one way of dressing," he once observed. Casually elegant in a blue man's shirt and denim skirt, Elena greeted me with the smiling openness that embodied Elaine Dundy's maxim that "charm is availability." Edmund appeared distracted, the long, sandy walk at seventy-six seeming to have fortified his usual intimidating reserve. Nonetheless, I plunged in.

"Edmund!" I exclaimed, "you'll never guess who's here on the beach—*Dwight*'s here!" Wilson didn't react, while continuing to slowly advance, stick in hand. "My father, Dwight," I needlessly explained, this time drawing forth what Paul Horgan, in his memoir, *Tracings*, nicely renders as Wilson's fits-all-occasions response of "M'ym." Worn out, he seemed to be taking nothing in until he was a few feet from Dwight's prone, book-absorbed back. Then Wilson hurried ahead up on pale, spindly legs, raised his black cane with violent authority, and bellowed, "MMMM'YYYYMMMM!!"

"Edmund!" Dwight leapt up like a startled mouse, then collapsed in red-faced delight. Chuckling contentedly, my father's friend plopped down beside him.

"I gather you've been looking into Poe," began the man who had helped revive Poe's reputation in 1943. "Now tell me, Dwight. . . ."

Edmund Wilson, dour in dress and the grand man of American letters, but not above some gaslight camping, was also a man of the world. Rising in the afternoon after a long night in his study among, say, the eighty-six volumes of Michelet he examined to write the vivid chapters that open *To the Finland Station*, Wilson might work in his pajamas and dressing gown. When he appeared in this industrious dishabille at the front door one day, he was teased by a Russian friend: "Why Edmund, you look like Oblomov!," a story he liked enough to tell on himself. The shy scholar could also smile when wounded. Perched atop the Newcomb's Hollow dunes with the Harry Levins one afternoon in 1951, Wilson entertained us with Cyril Connolly's review of *Memoirs of Hecate County*. "Now listen to this," he said, and then read aloud Connolly's dismissal of a "desiccated buffoon," treating the ripe vitriol with humor, though he would privately fume about this old friend's attack. On the eve of the great civil rights march to the Lincoln Memorial in 1963, Wilson chatted with two New Frontiersmen on Phillips Beach. Sitting just below the dunes, far from the other bathers, he sifted sand from hand to hand like an hourglass while talking with Arthur Schlesinger and Arthur's houseguest, Richard Goodwin. Suddenly, two monarch butterflies went all atangle in the air, attracting the

amateur naturalist who had studied tiny toads in a ter-
rarium at Money Hill. "Oh, look at those butterflies,"
Edmund Wilson laughed. "They're . . . they're copulat-
ing! Volodya [Nabokov] would love this!"

For all of Wilson's delight in tangling butterflies, his
formality, his reticence, and the credentials of an Enlightenment polymath like Voltaire or Dr. Johnson
made him intimidating on my many visits to Money
Hill to see his son, Reuel. At five foot six and two hundred pounds, Wilson was a compact, formidable version of the formidable Sydney Greenstreet. Also daunting was his cross-examination style of conversation and
what an admiring Alfred Kazin described as "that
hoarse, heavily breathing voice box," which could make
Edmund seem "apoplectic, stiff, out of breath." Then
there was Wilson's drinking and domestic quarreling,
and the less well-known way he coolly documented his
sexual practices with Elena in diaries written for pos-
terity. These, coupled with the scholarly reclusions of
the man who had learned Russian at forty, Hebrew in
his fifties, Hungarian in his sixties, and was getting up
Old Church Slavonic and Welsh at the time of his
death at seventy-seven, made Wilson sometimes trying. While always on his best behavior with me as
Reuel's friend, Edmund Wilson remained a remote figure, increasing his grandeur in my eyes.

Most of this remoteness reflected the strenuous work
regimes of the man who alerted America to Hemingway in 1924, then to Eliot, Joyce, Proust, and Yeats via
Axel's Castle in 1931, convinced Mary McCarthy to
write fiction in 1938, and almost single-handedly reviv-
ed Scott Fitzgerald's reputation in the '40s—simulta-

neously promoting an unknown Vladimir Nabokov. After all this, he wrote major books on the Dead Sea Scrolls and the literature of the Civil War, was the *New Yorker*'s literary critic for almost two decades, and did multicultural studies long before their vogue. Hidden labors sustained the forthright, conversational style with which Wilson engaged his reader in his broadsides against detective stories, in repellent subjects like de Sade or unpromising ones like mushrooms, as well as in much of the Western literary canon, keeping one at his side for scores of pages in an endless, colorful quest. To work up so many topics, often from one of the many foreign languages he knew, then write about them in what W. H. Auden admired as Wilson's "clear-window" prose, meant many reclusions for the man who relieved them by mastering a book titled *150 Ways to Play Solitaire*.

"THE Minotaur" was the unaffectionate nickname for Wilson between Mary McCarthy and her next husband, Bowden Broadwater—"the poor minotaur in his maze," dependent on the sacrifice of maidens like McCarthy. If the Minotaur seems a bit much, Wilson, the ferocious workaholic, often seemed buried in a labyrinth at Money Hill, at the end of a hallway lined by tall black ledger notebooks holding his lively journal accounts which became *The Twenties*, *The Thirties*, *The Forties*, *The Fifties*, and the final flowering of *The Sixties*, virtually an autobiographical novel about a rich worldly and scholarly life. Sometimes from that long hallway's far end, a distant bellow would rise as Reuel and I had lunch with Elena in the kitchen: we'd giggle, while Elena was soon off with Edmund's lunch tray. Flaubert, like Wilson fond of gossip, travel, and the voluminous accumulation of knowledge that he'd satirize in *Bouvard and Pécuchet*, engaged in such lonely and creative hibernations at his old family home on the Meuse, tirelessly refining his prose with his "two hundred pens," as the self-styled "Bear of Crois-set." "The Minotaur of Money Hill" followed in this industrious tradition, affirming his privacy with the famous postcard sent to various importuners covering almost all the commonplaces of literary commerce. "Edmund Wilson regrets that it is impossible for him to . . . ," the card begins, followed by a list from "read manuscripts" to "supply opinions on literary or other subjects," a neat check mark beside whichever item was apt. This nose-thumb was long before the cultural hyperbole of talk shows, newspaper Living Sections, or State Councils on the Arts: a splendid bit of literary bad manners from a time when another Massachusetts legend, across the Bay in Fenway Park, had refused to tip his cap to the crazed stands after homering in his last time ever at bat. As John Updike explained, "Gods don't answer fan mail." And like another contemporary nonpareil, Groucho Marx, Wilson was leery of any club that wanted him. "When one is *someone*, why should one want to be *something*?" asked Flaubert about the French Academy. "Not to have been a member is the only distinction in my life that I can be sure of," wrote Wilson about the American Academy of Arts and Letters.

While shunning academies, Wilson took notes on the world: *The Sixties* interweaves New York literary gossip, travel notes from Hungary and Israel, musings on his beloved Talcottville, and meetings with a global network of literary friends, from Auden in New York and Isaiah Berlin at Oxford to Malraux in Paris or Nabokov in Montreux. In Wellfleet, however, Wilson was somewhat invisible. Given his heavy work regimen at this home base, I rarely saw him beyond his occasional appearances at the big lawn parties with which Gilbert Seldes opened and closed the Cape season on the Fourth of July and Labor Day. Even Wilson's swimming routines were seldom observed. While amusing us with "desiccated buffooneries" at Newcomb's Hollow, Edmund sat atop the dunes, far above a mobbed public beach. His favorite freshwater bathing was at the tiny, claustral Spectacle Pond, his accounts of its seclusion and seasonal changes memorable in both *The Forties* and *The Fifties*. One afternoon, at a suitably obscure beach on the vast, popular Gull Pond, I observed Wilson's singular swimming style, what he called a "one-arm treadle." In this unique semicrawl his right arm propelled him and his left arm stabilized his body. Now and then, he raised his large head to gasp air like a surfacing whale, before resuming a head-down, straight-on progress, one rigid arm sawing the air like an odd kind of swimming machine. Emulating my hero, I tried the treadle—and gulped down a sizable portion of Gull Pond.

Reinforcing Wilson's seclusion was a patrician disdain for cars. When Mary McCarthy won a Chevrolet in a local raffle, it became a symbol of independence from their housebound routine, a symbol that rankled after the divorce, when she sold it to Dwight for a dollar—producing a lively scene after we ran into Wilson on a path to Gull Pond. "I hear you're driving my car this summer," he plunged in. "But Edmund," father protested in his maddeningly genial way. "I bought it from Mary for a dollar and she won it in that raffle." "But *I* gave her the money for the raffle ticket!" And that was that. Later that summer, as we drove up for a party at Joan Colebrook's in the old Dos Passos house on Truro's bayberry moors, "Our car began to smoke," my mother recalls, "and Wilson, leaving Joan's party, again made his remark about it being 'My car.'" Quite a claim, given our Chevy's decrepit belchings in Joan's driveway! But that George Price jalopy had been Mary's potential thread out of the labyrinth at Money Hill: to see it driven by Dwight, who had taken her side!

THAT the next Mrs. Wilson was another patrician at first meant the extravagant hiring of local taxi driver Bill Peck as a virtual family chauffeur. "Mr. Peck," as Elena respectfully called him, was a gentle, reserved Yankee in his late fifties who met Wilson dress codes with a bow tie, white shirt, and Sam Snead straw hat. His car was a gleaming, forest green Buick with light gray seats and a limousine's quiet ride. Mr. Peck endlessly ferried the Wilsons about, also driving Edmund to Talcottville every summer: no meter ticked on those long trips to upstate New York, but the bills were staggering. Eventually, Elena rebelled. Given Money Hill's profligacies in food and drink, from prime cuts to the best brands, she took on its biggest waste with driving lessons, then purchased a car.

To Edmund's cool moon, Elena was a radiant sun. A wonderful blend of Old World chic and New World brio, Elena Mumm Wilson combined sex appeal and maternity, femininity and feminism. Mary McCarthy's fictional take on Elena as a doormat hausfrau in *A Charmed Life* reveals a certain jealousy. Elena was, admittedly, dedicated to Edmund's creature comforts: on her lunch tray for the busy bellower down the hall might be a minute steak on toast, a salad, buttered Portuguese bread warmed in the oven, gleaming family silver, a linen napkin. More memorable, however, was the lively cosmopolitan and activist. The daughter of a German and a White Russian, her paternal side founding Mumm's champagne, her maternal grandfather the tsar's ambassador to America and Japan, she was raised by an English governess and grew up in a townhouse near Frankfurt, as well as hotel suites in Paris and Switzerland. Fluent in English, French, German, and Russian, she was an invaluable helpmate to a polylingual explorer. I recall the Wilsons reading Proust together in the early '60s; the winter of 1965 finds Edmund noting how, "in the evening, we have drinks and read *Faust*. . . . the fireplace in the middle room has contributed a lot to our coziness." Elena was also involved in various Cape causes, from saving Provincetown's harbor to Gerry Studds's long-shot insurgency in a congressional district that hadn't gone Democratic since the Gilded Age. As the turbulence of the '60s grew, she remained an unwavering, sensible, Adlai Stevenson lib-

eral. Her cultural and political interests make it fitting
that Elena's monument to Edmund would be his *Letters on Literature and Politics*, which she reconstructed
from the meager starting point of four carbons at
Money Hill.

Meeting with someone doing an oral history on Mary
McCarthy, I spent a lot of time discussing Elena, for
outside of my family, few adults had given me such intelligent, flattering attention in my youth. As our mu-
tual interest in politics grew during the '60s, we often
spoke of strategies and events at the Phillips Beach or
over a drink at Money Hill. Sipping a Scotch, Elena
would puff away on a cigarette and laugh in her husky,
yet feminine, way. Raised, amused eyebrows accompanied declarations: "Now *Mike. Really.* That fellow
Nixon is beyond *belief.*" Once voted one of Europe's
ten most glamorous women, in her usual casual dress
Elena would sprawl rangily on her throne, a low, wide
powder blue couch in the middle room near Edmund's
study, the "blue room." Some of the blueness came
from home economies by a continental lady versed in
the old domestic arts, Elena dying white quilts with
bluing to cover sofas, chairs. More blueness appeared
in two superb marine oil sketches by Edwin Dickinson.
Edmund's one, rather unusual, contribution to the blue
room appeared in white lines on windows looking out
on a small brick patio bordered by hedges—poems
etched into the panes. The master of clear-window
prose had poetic windows, as friends like Auden, Louise Bogan, Nabokov, Dorothy Parker, or Stephen
Spender used a diamond-tipped stylus to inscribe their

verse in the glass at Money Hill and Talcottville. Vandals broke Bogan's and Spender's panes but spared an Elizabeth Bishop poem discovered there by Roger Straus, which existed nowhere else.

THE lifeless living room up front was where we children played cards or Monopoly while listening to Edmund's folk, opera, pop, and vaudeville records, like Hilde Gueden's coy "Laughing Song" from *Fledermaus* or Spike Jones's "Cocktails for Two." Or there was Willie Howard's ripe agitation in Union Square, promising things like jobs and decent housing for all Americans, promises that remain unmet today, embroidering each pledge with "And comes the revolution, comrades, we'll *all* have strawberries and cream!" "But I don't *like* strawberries and cream," whines an adenoidal spoilsport. How we loved this rude takeoff on poster art, and how amusing to hear this Left-Jewish humor in that WASP parlor with its Federal mahogany pieces. Between that unused parlor and the blue room's hearth, a small dining room was dominated by a round mahogany table set with blue Staffordshire. Here was where Reuel and I deployed a whoopee cushion to confound the portly master of the house, slipping the famous instrument of childhood humor beneath his usual seat cushion before a Sunday lunch. Presiding over a roast, roast potatoes, and what he jauntily called "the broc," Wilson sat down heavily—in silence. Had he been too much for our inflated rubber pancake? Exploding in giggles, we showed our puzzled nonvictim the flat pink joke. He responded with a laugh, rewarding our youthful initiative for effort anyway.

Mainly, however, Edmund stayed in his study, so we'd beard the Minotaur in his lair, creeping along the driveway outside, then jumping up with a shout, to some perfunctory "Mmm'yyymmms." We'd needlessly flee to the barn out back, a fragrant remnant from Money Hill's farmhouse origins. Amidst the hayloft's horsey smells, we'd devise what Dwight described in a letter to Mary McCarthy as "expeditions, mostly of a punitive kind, to spy upon and harass various older persons." To a child, Edmund Wilson was largely that imposing figure who poked his head into the kitchen in search of his tray, sending a pleasant "M'ym" or two my way before retiring to his sanctum down the hall, a sanctum so inviolable that, even when Edmund was off in Talcottville, it was a space crossed quickly as a short-cut to the enclosed back stairs to Reuel's room, leaving one with the impression of a rather neat library in a gentleman's club.

So it was an event one afternoon in 1953, when Edmund invited us into his study to hear some new additions to his pop archives, prefaced by brief intro-ductions. There was a wonderful album by the com-poser-guitarist Henri Salvador, which I promptly bought, then wore out at Exeter. There was some Piaf: a first hearing of what we'd later enjoy at Harvard on the Club Casablanca's cosmopolitan jukebox. Above all, there was Sinatra's landmark album, *Wee Small Hours of the Morning*, part of his famous comeback that year. Suddenly, the boyish Voice of '40s bobby-soxers was the "hip" Chairman on the album's cover—porkpie hat tilted back, Windsor knot at half-mast, cigarette smoke idly curling up. This was also the first "theme" LP,

building a mood over many cuts—and putting Edmund
in the vanguard of pop trends, where he remained. Six
years later, I ran into Reuel, crossing the Cambridge
Common with a birthday present for Edmund, who
was lecturing at Harvard from his drafts of the chapters
for *Patriotic Gore*. The gift was an album by a new
singer named Bobby Short, elegant in gray flannels,
head thrown back and striding on a cheeky, confident
cover—as Edmund Wilson kept up with breakthroughs
in saloon singing.

THE previous year, Reuel and I had driven down from
Cambridge for a November weekend at Money Hill.
Leafless trees made the woods transparent around my
closed home on Slough Pond; a brisk wind blew up
Newcomb's Hollow as we walked with Elena on a
bright, deserted beach. Over drinks in the blue room,
Edmund was in an expansive mood. As an early fall
sunset raised the white etched lines on his poetic
windows, he sat on his little sofa across from Elena's
powder blue chair and laid out cards on a coffee table.
"Now here's a little trick I picked up at Harrah's Club
in Reno," he began, like a good entertainer. Cards and
magic fascinated Wilson, he and Edwin O'Connor
sometimes traveling together to attend magicians' conventions. While the devout Catholic novelist probably
enjoyed magic for its own, secular sake, his atheist
companion, as Reuel has observed, regarded magic as
a parareligion suited to his rationalist's mind, being
supremely confident of the human ingenuity behind
Oz's curtain. That night, over after-dinner drinks,
Edmund regaled us with '20s memories of Dos Passos

and Parker, Croly and Cowley. Then he rose abruptly, back to business. "And now, I must read some Dickens to Helen," he announced, leaving for his young daughter's room. I think it was *Copperfield*.

After Harvard, Reuel moved away and I rarely saw Edmund beyond chance meetings like that amusing encounter with Dwight on the beach in 1971. A few months later, during a family Thanksgiving on Slough Road, I dropped by Money Hill for tea with Elena. As I was leaving, she asked if I'd like to see Edmund. So I walked down the long hall from the kitchen, through that neat men's club library of a study—and into a small side room that had been converted into a bedroom during Wilson's recent illness. Edmund was slumped in a worn blue armchair in the cozy, well-lit room. He looked frail, his white eyebrows seemed more prominent in his sunken face. In his light gray pajamas and salmon bathrobe, Edmund Wilson was recovering from a cold, clutching a handkerchief but, as always, working. On a side table beside his lunch tray was the typescript for his new introduction to the seventeenth edition of *To the Finland Station*, in which Wilson admitted to writing "a much too amiable portrait of Lenin" back in 1940.

I had just finished E. H. Carr's *Romantic Exiles*, so our conversation moved easily from *Finland Station* to Carr's account of Russian political expatriates like the Herzens during the post-Decembrist era. It was gratifying, for once, to keep up with the literary pace of my formidable idol. Having noted the Herzens' close relations with another exile, the German revolutionary poet Georg Herwegh, Edmund asked if I'd read *The*

Possessed. I hadn't. "Well, you really must read it," he urged, "to see how Herzen's moderate form of radicalism was succeeded by the nihilism of the *narodniki.*" Indeed Stavrogin's circle of crazies, I'd soon discover, resembled the Weathermen lately sprung from the ashes of our own hopes for reform. After a few minutes on *The Possessed*, Wilson slumped back in his chair, his pale face flushed. I headed for the door. As I reached the threshold, Edmund bellowed, softly, "Now see here, Mike. . . . Did you *really* read *The Romantic Exiles*? Or were you just making all of that up?" Assured that I had—and yet hadn't—he motioned me back to the seat beside his armchair. "In that case, sit down for a minute. Now let me tell you what I think *really* happened between the Herzens and Herwegh in Geneva. Now I don't think that Carr got it right at all. . . ."

REVISITING THE
CRITIC ON
THE SCROLLS

JAMES A. SANDERS

I HAVE grown up with the Dead Sea Scrolls. I was a fledgling instructor in Rochester, in upstate New York where Wilson returned at the end of his life, when his first stunning articles on the scrolls appeared in the *New Yorker* in 1955. I met Wilson ten years later, when he was kind enough to consult me before going to Israel. Rereading him on the scrolls has been like reliving the formative years of my professional life. On first reading these essays forty years ago, I recall thinking how much he did not get quite right, and how his point of view sometimes seemed slanted according to whom he was quoting or with whom he had had conversations. By contrast, when read today his work seems not only engrossing and enthralling but also amazingly balanced and fair, given the fact that he was a self-avowed antireligionist. Once I thought that Wilson was overly influenced by one of my own teachers, André Dupont-Sommer of the École des Hautes Études in Paris, and by John Allegro of the University of Manchester. While Dupont-Sommer was a far more serious scholar than Allegro, they both found in the early published scrolls as much evidence as they could against the traditionally understood origins of Christianity—in fact, considerably more than was there, as Dupont-Sommer eventually, not long before his death, came to acknowledge. But reading Wilson now forty years later, I find that, while their anti-Christian stances clearly interested him personally, as a professional he always sought to put their views in the contexts of the fuller dialogues of the time.

As I revisit Wilson about those days, I experience a respect I frankly did not have as a young scholar needing to keep his credentials polished. Time and again, while Wilson found his way through the claims and counterclaims about the significance of the scrolls, he came down on the side of issues that time has vindicated. In his engaging discussion of the Copper Scroll from Qumran Cave Three, he admits he preferred John Allegro's fanciful view of the treasures listed as having been actual, immense amounts of gold, silver, and precious stones over J. T. Milik's understanding that the scroll was part of an ancient literary genre of fabled wealth, though he knew from Allegro himself that Milik was "perhaps the most brilliant of our little team of scroll editors." He adopted Frank Cross's idea that the scrolls and fragments in the Qumran caves formed in antiquity a discrete library that belonged to a Jewish sect of the time, as opposed to the other theories being advanced. And that theory has indeed proven the most enduring. There is yet today only one serious challenge to the library theory, though a sizable group of scholars now questions whether the community which owned the library were the Essenes, the view of W. F. Albright, which Cross, his student, has vigorously defended. Nonetheless, Wilson's careful reading of Pliny, Philo, and Josephus about the ancient Essenes still commands respect as a general account of the topic. He saw the importance of the scrolls in understanding what he called "intertestamental Judaism" and the beginnings of Christianity.

Wilson also studied Hebrew. At the beginning of the essay entitled "On First Reading Genesis," a delight in itself, he tells of going through the attic of his mother's house in upstate New York and finding the Hebrew Bible as well as a Hebrew grammar and dictionary that had belonged to his grandfather, a Presbyterian minister. He was "piqued a little at the thought" that his grandfather could read something he could not; so in 1952 he enrolled in a course in Hebrew at Princeton Seminary, where his grandfather had graduated a little over a century earlier, in 1846—and where Wilson himself first became interested in the Dead Sea Scrolls. His reading of Genesis, from a lingering Presbyterian perspective, is filled with naively wonderful observations about Hebrew morphology and syntax. Such was the indomitable curiosity that drove him to learn as much as he could about this curious world. As he poignantly put it in a postscript to *Red, Black, Blond and*

Olive, "We have then to try to know what we are and what we are doing on this earth."

Quite taken with the fact that Hebrew, like other Semitic languages, lacks Western cultural and linguistic understandings of time but rather has verbs that speak of either the completeness or the incompleteness of an action, Wilson calls Hebrew a "timeless language." He compares it to Russian, which in his reading as well as his early travels in the Soviet Union, had suggested to him the Russian concept of time, or lack of same. "We live with history as religious civilizations lived with God, and behind our conception of history is our special conception of time," he concludes. "This sense of transcendent principle has always had to be corrected by the realistic observation, the practical worldliness of the Greco-Roman tradition. It is the reciprocal relation of the two that has made what there is of our civilization." It seems to me that Wilson was perhaps the ultimate intellectual product of the Greco-Roman tradition of free inquiry and deep suspicion of the transcendent.

Among the most engaging passages in his enlarged book about the scrolls are those in which he reports visits with prominent personalities, especially those with Yigael Yadin, David Flusser, and Teddy Kolleck. He was quite taken with Professor Flusser's well-known erratic genius. After a particularly delightful report of a visit with Flusser, Wilson writes, "The thing about Flusser is that he flusses." He was also taken with S. Y. Agnon, saturated as the latter was with the learning of the Bible, Talmud, and Kabbala. He saw

how Agnon, like most Jewish writers since the time of
Ezra and Nehemiah, wrote scripturally; or as Wilson
put it, "the larding of literature with ancient quotations
has long been a feature of Hebrew writing." Wilson's
perceptiveness demands quotation: "Jewish self-mock-
ery, tragic in its implications, this drollery that is
also moral," he writes, "goes back to the first great de-
feat at the hands of the Babylonians, the impotence for
action, the minority status, that this for a time imposed.
It is, in any case, very old, the irony which still gives its
accent to Agnon and to the Yiddish humorists. For the
Jew, the fundamental irony is that God should have
made him promises of special protection and favor, and
then have allowed him to suffer a succession of crush-
ing disasters."

Wilson's commentary is fortifying to me, to use a
word he sometimes uses. "It has always been of the essence of the Jewish genius that it works through the
spirit and the intellect, that, in spite of the importance
to the Jews of such names as Jerusalem and Zion, it
does not need a habitation other than the souls of
men," he believes, thus paying tribute to "the affirmation of the power of the human spirit in touch with its
divine source and independent of place and condition."
Yet this same observer shrewdly concludes that "the
return of the Jews to their country of origin, the rever-
sion to their ancient language and, with these, a certain
relaxation—in the sense that a steel spring may be
said to relax from bending—into their habits of self-
sufficiency, has made it possible for them to stand alone
and not to worry about pleasing some dominant 'race';

digging themselves in has set them free, with the result—but superficially a paradox—that the Jews seem
in Israel less different instead of more different from
other people." Thus the critic celebrates the intellectual and moral stamina of the human race; and it is useful for me, at my age, to return to this, savoring the
wisdom of a man I briefly knew in my youth.

THE WRITING
AND ACTING OF
HISTORY

WILSON'S LENIN

DAVID REMNICK

EDMUND WILSON'S forays into Soviet Russia, despite
his inimitable style and curiosity, were accompanied
by the dubious judgments of his era and his circle. It's
not impossible to imagine what even Mikhail Gorbachev might make of *To the Finland Station*. (Alas, this
is a purely imaginative act; Wilson is not read in
contemporary Russia.) Gorbachev and other erstwhile
Communists would surely recognize the outline of *To
the Finland Station*—its accretion of authors rising to
the pinnacle of Marx and Engels, Lenin, and Trotsky—
as an almost exact replica of a statue in the Alexander
Gardens outside the Kremlin, a kind of totem-pole of
theorists and thinkers, from the early socialists to Lenin
the great. Gorbachev would surely recognize the way
that Wilson understands the writing of history as an
essential political act and even a weapon, and would
admit the outsized role of history in Soviet politics.
Wilson, for his part, would have relished the fact that
the fiercest debates in the Politburo at the beginning

of the so-called radicalized perestroika in 1987 were not over economic policy, which was hopelessly muddled, or foreign policy, which Gorbachev and Edward Shevardnadze decided more or less by diktat, but rather over the question of history. In the regime's final attempt to portray its own history, it came down to: Do we or do we not publish Grossman, Orwell, Nabokov, Solzhenitsyn? What do we say about Bukharin? Can we as a party survive and still let on that Lenin was no god?

Wilson would have found the transcripts of those debates—some of them are published in Gorbachev's recent memoir—painful and delicious. He would have enjoyed their obvious comedy—party hacks, former factory heads, lifelong apparatchiks deciding the fate of an empire on the basis of an essentially scholastic question. One can only guess how painful he would have found the headaches these poor men had, because Wilson in his time—and here we get to the nub of it—had, if only as an American and as a literary critic, made some of the very same mistakes. He too romanticized Lenin. He too saw what he chose to see when he walked the streets of Moscow. While he was mistakenly hardheaded about Kafka in *Classics and Commercials* and Wallace Stevens in *The Shores of Light*, he turned to mush before the great Ilyich.

The temptation in our era of liberal triumphalism, some of it justified, some of it not, is to do to Edmund Wilson what Paul Hollander did to him and to so many others in *Political Pilgrims*—that is, to collect his more ridiculous quotations, rip them out of context, and beat him like a drum. Here is a typical and absurd description of Moscow picked out by Mr. Hollander from Wilson's Soviet journal in 1935: "One gradually comes to realize that though the people's clothes are dreary, there is little, if any, destitution. Although there are no swell parts of the city, there are no degraded parts either. There are no shocking sights on the streets, no down-and-outers, no horrible diseases, no old people picking in garbage pails. I was never able to find anything like a slum or any quarter that even seemed dirty." This is not a difficult game to play. Consider this passage from the chapter of *Finland Station* on Lenin called "The Great Headmaster":

> If he gravitated into the role of dictator, it was because the social physics of Russia made it inevitable that he should do so. In his drive toward personal domination, there was nothing of the egoism of genius or of the craving for honor of the statesman. Lenin was one of the most selfless of great men. He did not care about seeing his name in print, he did not want people to pay him homage, he did not care about how he looked, he had no pose of not caring about it. He regarded his political opponents not as competitors who were to be crushed but as colleagues he had regrettably lost, collaborators he had failed to recruit. Unlike certain of the other great revolutionists, Marx or Bakunin, for example, he is imaginable as a statesman of the West, developing in a different tradition.

Lenin, as Wilson could not have known then but
should at some point have admitted, was the inventor
of the concentration camp on the European continent;
Lenin also preceded Stalin in his murderous assault
on the intelligentsia, the "kulaks," the Russian Orthodox Church and all organized religion, and any other
"enemies of the revolution." The legacy of Ilyich was
neither liberty nor prosperity, but rather a regime that
sustained itself on murder and finally disintegrated and
collapsed in 1991. Wilson, like so many intellectuals of
his time, made many foolish judgments, such as reject-
ing André Gide's hardheaded reconsideration of the
Soviet experience in *Return to the USSR*, calling it
nothing more than "characteristic of Gide's perversity."
Despite his own romance with Moscow, Walter Benjamin, a far more complex Marxist, saw many things
there that Wilson did not or at any rate could not admit
at the time.

If this was the case, the primary reason, I believe, is
rooted in biography and the circumstances of Wilson's
attraction to Russia. Just after finishing *Axel's Castle*, a
project both literary and journalistic, Wilson immersed
himself as a reporter in the conditions of the country
during the Depression. He traveled, pad in hand, to
the Ford factory in Detroit, to scenes of rural poverty
and miner's strikes in Kentucky, to the Scottsboro
Boys' rape case trial in Tennessee. He did this not
merely out of sympathy and interest or duty but also
out of a sense of freelance urgency. He doubtless
hoped the book he got out of all this would sell. Wilson
was quite poor, nearly always at the edge of financial

failure. His accent may have been that of Mrs. Roose-velt or Julia Child, but his circumstances were dire. Money was a furious emotional battle for him—we needn't wait for the IRS crisis in the early '60s to know that.

A vivid sense of class and a muted fury is everywhere in his American reporting. Wilson wrote about his travels and the chaos around him in the tones of a converting leftist—that is, with a certain degree of glee. As he said in "The Literary Consequences of the Crash," looking back in 1952, "one couldn't help being exhilarated at the sudden unexpected collapse of that stupid, gigantic fraud." He saw the time not as one of possible practical reform, as liberals would then and at later moments of crisis, but rather as a time of what the Russians call *perelom*, a breakthrough, a possibility of a new world. Like Dreiser, Dos Passos, and a number of other writers, Wilson voted for Foster in 1932; he voted for Norman Thomas in 1936, 1940, 1944, and 1948. He wanted nothing to do with FDR. He engaged left-wing politics without losing a sense of mandarin hauteur. Mike Gold mocked Wilson's in-creasing devotion to leftist causes and ideology, saying that he ascended the proletarian bandwagon with the "arrogance of a myopic, high-bosomed Beacon Hill ma-tron entering a common street car." There is some truth in that, though mainly on the level of style and personal carriage.

Wilson went to Russia in May 1935, six months after the Kirov assassination and more than six years after the slaughter of the kulaks, determined to find an alternative, a worthy future not only for Russia and Europe but also for America. He traveled widely and long but not well—that is, not much better than George Bernard Shaw or Lincoln Steffens, who thought up the line "I've seen the future and it works," in advance of visiting Russia. In the preposterously titled *Travels in Two Democracies*, after wrestling with his darker impressions of the dictatorship, Wilson concluded that the Soviet Union was "the moral top of the world." This society, to him, represented a possible way out of the trying circumstances of American intellectuals, a fulfillment of an Enlightenment scenario that begins in history with Vico and ends with Lenin. Wilson's communism was—and I more than recognize the contradiction here—both conformist to its times and independent in spirit. He ignored, at any rate in his writing of that time, a letter from Dos Passos at Christmas 1934, describing the horror of the repression of the Kronstadt mutiny, the massacres in the Crimea, the exile of Trotsky, the persecution of the Social Revolutionaries, and the liquidation of the kulaks. I've already mentioned his dismissal of Gide. On the other hand, to make the picture more complicated, Wilson never joined the Communist Party and was quite disdainful of it. He attacked Malcolm Cowley for rationalizing the sham purge trials of 1937–38, and declared, "Stalin is hopelessly reactionary and corrupt."

In some high-level way, I think, in his early mistakes Wilson fell victim to a peculiarly journalistic syndrome that existed then and now. Journalists, especially on a major foreign story, often show the same independence

of mind as a pack of wolves driven to meat. They tend
to empathize with a figure or a class, and the coverage
reflects this. There is no ideological pattern. We have
seen American reporters being oversympathetic with
the Sandinistas in Nicaragua and at the same time sympathetic with Russian monetarists such as Yuri Gaidar
in 1992, or with right-wing Catholic intellectuals in Po-
land. Journalists as a class are given to this romanticism, and I think Wilson was too. Wilson's greatest romance was not with the idea of the Russian Politburo
member but with that of the Russian intellectual. He,
like so many before and after him, was jealous of the
place of Russian literature and the Russian literary man
in Russian society. He did not yet understand, at least
in the '30s, that the supreme artists of the time, Akhma-
tova, Mandelstam, and so on, were not exalted in the
eyes of the regime but demonized. They were meat for
the grinder. Wilson, unlike his more experienced
friend, Isaiah Berlin, suffered from identifying with the
wrong Russian intellectuals; his heroes were political
idealists in the populist-Marxist tradition. A third reason for Wilson's difficulties is that while a spectacular
reader of literature, he was an all-too-human reader of
power and politics. His work never engages very well
the connections between theory and its consequences,
between that which he sees joyfully—the written
word—and that which he sees only dimly—the coming
of the gulag. Because he makes of Lenin a sort of aesthetic object when he describes him in his tomb at the
end of *Travels in Two Democracies*, he also fails to confront the other great question of Soviet history, the

connection between Lenin and Stalin, the connection between the inventor of terror and camps and their supreme artist. In *To the Finland Station* we never hear of the Lenin who could write a telegram saying "Shoot more professors."

Wilson's were the errors of a time, a place, and a temperament, and it should be noted that many of his contemporaries did worse and persisted in their mistaken judgments far longer. Wilson fully acknowledged his errors in his preface to the 1972 edition of *To the Finland Station*. "We did not foresee that the New Russia must contain a good deal of the Old Russia: censorship, secret police, the entanglements of bureaucratic incompetence, and so on," he wrote.

> This book of mine assumes throughout that an important step in progress has been made, that a fundamental breakthrough had occurred, that nothing in our human history would ever be the same again. I had no premonition that the Soviet Union was to become one of the most hideous tyrannies that the world had ever known, and Stalin the most cruel and unscrupulous of the merciless Russian czars. The book should therefore be read as a basically reliable account of what the revolutionists thought they were doing in the interests of "a better world." Some corrections and modifications ought, however, to be made here to rectify what was on my part a too hopeful bias. What was permanently valuable—whatever that implies—in the October Revolution I cannot pretend to estimate.

Outside of Gide's extensive exercise in revision, *Return to the U.S.S.R.*, I can think of no major author who has written a more thorough renunciation of the premise of an earlier but mature work. Wilson does it here in a preface, but it must have been a painful exercise all the same. It had to be equally painful to go back, in the '50s, to his Soviet journal and interpolate in brackets all the experiences and impressions he had suppressed in 1935, so as not to get his friends into trouble or to put too much emphasis on details he "regarded then as inessential." The result is an extraordinary document, published in *Red, Black, Blond and Olive*, that sets the fellow traveler of 1935 beside the veteran of the age of totalitarian states, who can imagine his friend the critic D. S. Mirsky being dragged from the "almost Dostoevskian lodgings" where the two had dined on cheap caviar and cucumbers and discussed literature, and sent off to the goldfields where he died insane. Rather than cast a censorious eye on Wilson at the Finland station, I prefer to see the episode in its entirety as further proof of Wilson's integrity as a writer and as a witness to his times. As Nietzsche writes in one of his notebooks, "The courage of one's convictions is almost nothing. The real courage is to change those convictions."

THE INDEPENDENT
RADICAL OBSERVER

DANIEL AARON

EDMUND WILSON was not an acute political diagnosti-
cian, a student of comparative government, or an econ-
omist. He was, besides his many other talents, a good,
and sometimes inspired, journalist who reported accurately what he saw and heard and thought. One of his
observations about Turgenev applies equally well, I
think, to himself. Turgenev, he said, "sticks to his objective judgment, his line of realistic criticism, his
resolve to stand free of movements, to rise above personalities, to recognize all points of view that have any
sincerity or dignity." This isn't to say that Wilson's political reportage, especially in the '20s and the '30s, was
disinterested. Like many American intellectuals during
and after the big stock market crash, he thought capitalism was kaput and its managers incompetent knaves
and betrayers of the old republican values. But even in
the heady days before Roosevelt's election, when he
was cataloguing national blemishes in *American Jitters*,

he remained leery of collective enterprises, indeed of all constraining formulas. And although in 1932 he rallied support for the Communists, it was because he believed Communists were the only ones with a plan and a will to effect the plan. He didn't relish their company or their tactics. He came to regard the Party as a kind of enthusiastical church whose imported political vocabulary, toiling masses, dictatorship of the proletariat, and the like grated on his ears, and whose true believers consisted largely of "queer, equivocal, anomalous people." At best it might serve as a useful irritant and a vehicle to put fundamental questions before the public; at no time, as David Remnick says, did he indicate the slightest intention of joining the Party.

The story of Wilson's political oscillations has been told many times and with different emphases, depending on the writer, but perhaps not enough attention has been paid to the extrapolitical considerations. And I have something in mind that has more to do with temperament or disposition—I mean his ambivalent feeling toward his family and class, toward the old rotten system that he saw crumbling before him. I mean his strenuous efforts to break away from the values and prejudices of most of the people he had grown up with, and his personal tolerance for these same people whose ideas and styles of life offended him. I also mean his education and the schools he attended, above all the books that powerfully influenced him. And finally, the impact of his military experiences in World War I, his exposure to hospitals, his discovery as an enlisted man of ordinary working-class Americans. These experiences, I believe, turned him against subsequent wars, even the American Civil War, and had something to do with his reasons for going to the Soviet Union.

On the eve of his trip to Russia, in May 1935, Wilson was an anticlerical positivist (strongly influenced in his youth by George Bernard Shaw and H. G. Wells), a celebrator of scientific genius, a humanist attuned to the shifts in high and popular culture, a staunch partisan of democratic rights and intellectual freedom, a civic patriot in the style of John Jay Chapman, of whom he wrote very appreciatively. He was already a self-declared Marxist, although hardly an orthodox one. His Marx was less a Marxian than a humanist who drew proper distinctions between the modes of production and the "superstructure of higher activities," as Wilson put it, who indulged "the political shortcomings" of poets and rejected "any tendency to specialize art as a 'weapon.'" Marxism, Wilson's Marxism, in short, explained how such a favored son of a capitalist society could become a part of the dialectical process in order to undermine it. He went to Russia neither to worship nor to scoff but to give middle-class Americans a look at socialism in action. Neither then nor later did he hold up Russia as a model for the United States, but in 1935 he resolved to keep an open mind about its alleged iniquities.

Ostensibly, his reason for making the journey was to do research at the Marx-Engels Institute in Moscow and to complete his study of the words and actions of selected socialist worthies. The chance to inspect a new society and to have agreeable adventures was perhaps an even greater motive. In any event, his scholarly plans were scotched when, despite his efforts to stay clear of "all parties and special doctrines," he was suspected of being a crypto-Trotskyist and denied access to the Institute. Thus the traveler with no knowledge of Russian (a language he soon began to acquire) had to rely on his eyes and his hunches. Many pages in his Russian journal testify to his success in capturing the human and natural landscape as he perceived it, and registering his fluctuating moods. The journal, it must be said, also shows a man with the sketchiest knowledge of Russian history and culture making resounding pronouncements about a people he's just encountered and confidently shoring up his preconceptions. Some of them, listed by Simon Karlinsky in his introduction to the Wilson-Nabokov letters, he retained all his life.

The five months Wilson spent in the Soviet Union, including six weeks in a grungy Odessa hospital recovering from scarlatina, contain few startling insights. He liked the Russian people, their hunger for literature and the arts, their American-like informality, so different from the stiffness of the class-bound English. Still he had to confess "strange alternations of enthusiasm and disappointment." Nothing worked in the new Russia. Of course, according to his theory, that was the result of generations of oriental despotism and was to be expected. All the same, there were moments when the evasiveness, procrastination, and supineness of the population brought out, he wrote, "the Ivan the Terrible in all of us." This revealing comment has some

bearing on his admiration for Lenin, the social engineer
of Bolshevism—the amalgam, in Wilson's picture, of
the aristocrat, poet, and scientist—who grabbed his
benighted countrymen by the scruff of their collective
neck and forced them, as Wilson put it with unconscious irony, to recognize themselves as the masters
with the "power to create without fear whatever they
had in mind to imagine." Wilson could even famously
say that his transfigured hero had lifted Russia to the
moral top of the world. Documented revelations about
a different and all too earthly Lenin were years away
when Wilson wrote these words. Even so, the swelling
setpiece on the face of Lenin, a synecdoche of the will
of history that ends *Travels in Two Democracies*, is un-
expectedly rhapsodic.

When Wilson drove in a droshky to the Lenins'
family house in Ulanovsk, he was impressed by "its
sobriety and shining cleanness," its fine mahogany furniture, "its maps and music and books," the reassuring
artifacts of the cultivated middle class from which he
and, presumably, Lenin had derived. The side trip to
Ulanovsk fleshed out his conception of the Russian
gentry, whose appealing specimens he had encountered in the memoirs and fiction of Herzen, Turgenev,
Chekhov, and Tolstoy long before he was able to read
these authors in the original. They belonged to the
class he was most comfortable with at home or abroad
and blended harmoniously with his recollections of
an older America "where rather a high degree of civilization flourished against a background of pleasant
wildness."

Wilson played down the sinister aspects of Stalin's Russia. He didn't want to embarrass or endanger his contacts and was probably reluctant to provide ammunition for the anti-Soviet claque in America. He was too much the professional reporter, however, to stifle his reservations. What sticks in the mind are shots of listless, unsmiling crowds drifting along the shadeless, dirty walks in the Park of Culture and Rest, of the eating pavilion, with "the women in sneakers, the men without neckties, the shave-headed children" (Wilson never lost a kind of bourgeois fastidiousness) lining up for "bottles of pale wine and Soviet chocolates, slabs, spiral-piled on the bar." The Moscow tic—namely, the habit of looking over one's shoulder before venturing to say anything about politics—this, too, is registered. It is harder for him to explain away the pervasive dreariness of the Soviet scene, to palliate the condition of people so benumbed "by their own subhuman life of serfdom" that they've lost all capacity for enjoyment. Yes, they are poor, he concedes, but they aren't degraded. "There are no shocking sights on the streets, no down-and-outers, no horrible diseases, no old people picking in garbage pails," lame mitigations, as David Remnick has said, yet they don't drown out the undertone of disgust and exasperation to be heard in Wilson's Russian diary. It must have required considerable effort, one feels, for him to imagine the withering away of a state that imposed so many hard exactions on its population. What he objected to, sotto voce, in *Travels in Two Democracies*—the adoration of Stalin, the rubbing out of history, the arrogance of the trained and educated to-

ward their inferiors—gushed out not long after his return to the United States when, without equivocating,
he denounced the crimes of the corrupt and reactionary Stalinist officialdom and their American apologists.

Yet he hung on to old convictions. Twenty years
later, in *Patriotic Gore*, he attributed the degradation
of the great experiment chiefly to the persistence of
ancient national traits; not even Lenin's democratic
ideals, in Wilson's phrase, could root them out. Russia's
history furnished yet another example of the "tragic
contradiction between the right to peace and the
happiness of the ordinary man and the right to constructive domination by the state," the themes that
Pushkin had dramatized in "The Bronze Horseman," a
poem Wilson translated. Peter the Great broke a good
many eggs before he produced his omelet, and so, too,
did Lincoln, Bismarck, and Lenin, ruthless idealists
"of unusual intellect and formidable tenacity of character, of historical imagination, combined with powerful will." All three of them dispensed a bitter medicine
to their respective nations. Lenin spoke for the other
two as well as for himself when he called history a cruel
stepmother.

Wilson's exalting of Promethean life-bringers who
struggled to eliminate darkness and stagnation makes
him sound on occasion like an advocate of enlightened
coercion. Thus, in an amusing and slightly chilling
fable, the young critic pits the zoologist, emblem of
science and biological realism, against the sluggish
Galápagos iguana, indifferent to the future of his
species and content to doze for eternity in his burrow.

The zoologist can't persuade the iguana to join him in his quest to solve nature's mysteries, but he can force him to do so. The colloquy ends when the zoologist lassoes the iguana and carries him off by the tail. Comparing the doings of human beings with those of beasts and birds had sinister implications, Wilson admitted, but it suited his naturalistic bent and tempered his compassion for suffering humanity without, he had noted, lessening his sympathy for the dominated and the regimented.

By the late '30s, Wilson was pretty much convinced that writers like himself had no business intervening in politics. Their proper course was to put the situation on record in art. That did not mean, as he more than once enunciated, abandoning this world. The ivory tower he proposed for his metaphoric retirement resembled neither the iguana's comfortable burrow nor Axel's castle. It was a place for meditation—he used the French word *recueillement*—for the nourishment of the intellect, not an escape into fantasy. Wilson now looked back on the wrangling '30s with pain and irritation. How could anyone, he wondered, feel nostalgic for those mean and angry days? He felt much closer to the hopeful '20s, when the literary scene had seemed more lighthearted and politics less grim and demanding.

The bloom of his Russian adventure turned out to be the impetus it gave him to learn the Russian language, and most of all to acquaint himself with the poetry of Pushkin. He has been faulted, and justly so, I suppose, for imputing to himself an intimacy with Russian history and culture he didn't possess, but what other American literary critic of his time attempted with such eagerness and generosity to reach out to congenial minds and establish contact with a people whose cultural traditions and national characteristics puzzled, disturbed, and fascinated him until his death?

WILSON AND
SOVIET RUSSIA

A ROUNDTABLE

Michael Walzer: I would like to begin the discussion with a partial defense of *To the Finland Station* against the critique of David Remnick. I first read the book in 1953, when I was a freshman at college, and I admired every word of it. I read it with great excitement. It did not make me an apologist for the Soviet Union; in fact, I like to think it helped to make me an independent leftist and a critic of Stalinist politics. Listening to David Remnick read Edmund Wilson's self-critique of the early '70s, it seemed to me that there was something excessive about it, that he may have needed to say this but didn't quite tell the whole story about that book. When I reread *Finland Station* this past week, I found it a classic of the higher popularization—which was exactly what I needed coming from Johnstown, Pennsylvania, to college in 1953—a classic because of the internal tension the book sustains throughout its great flight. On the one hand, it's an epic history of the coming together of theory and practice, and that union represented and embodied in a very romanticized way—Lenin at the Finland station when, according to Wilson, "for the first time in the human exploit the key of a philosophy of history was to fit an historical lock." The key provided by this intellectual story that goes back to Vico was to fit the lock, Wilson wrote, himself knowing what was on the other side of the door. The story has that extraordinary, romantic moment near the end, when humanity seems on the eve of mastering its fate. But at the same time, at crucial points in the epic tale the reader is warned that things are going to turn out badly, and the sources of the coming despotism— not totalitarianism, he didn't have a sense of the full extent of the horror of the Russian regime and wasn't a participant in the left-sectarian Marxist debate out of which the theory of totalitarianism came—are carefully described, in the chapter on the dialectic, and in what is really a very fine critical analysis of Trotsky, of *Their Morals and Ours*. So the sense of hope with which the book ends and the foreknowledge of failure that is embedded in the prior narrative, that combination is somehow sustained, and it makes, I think, for a much better book than David Remnick acknowledges.

Daniel Aaron: Wilson began *Finland Station*, of course, before he went to Russia in 1935, and it wasn't finished until 1940. Thus it incorporated the experience of going to the Soviet Union and coming back. In the journals for the spring of 1934 is the comment "At some point during this rather sordid period, it occurred to me that nobody had ever presented in intelligible human terms the development of Marxism and other phases of the modern idea of history. I saw the possibilities of a narrative which would quite get away from the pedantic frame of theory." He knew, he said, that it would cause him a lot of trouble because he would have to learn German—he never really did learn it, I think—and Russian, and the project "would take me far afield of what I thought was my prime objective, a work of fiction made out of the materials that I had been compiling in these notebooks." Nonetheless he found himself excited by the challenge, and he went on. There is a novelistic and dramatic dimension about *Finland Station*. It has its heroes, its flawed heroes, its tragic failures, and there's something exhilarating in it, the sense of the power of the mind and these great leaders that really intoxicated him, and I think he still felt that even when finishing the work in a more realistic frame of mind.

David Remnick: Just to reply very briefly to Professor Walzer: I think Wilson's preface in 1972 is entirely appropriate, and too brutal neither on himself nor on his book. If in fact the tension about what is to come is embedded in *To the Finland Station*, it's only lightly embedded. It has none of the vividness of the romanticized portrait of Lenin or the more sophisticated account of Trotsky. Second, the emphasis on what might go wrong in his writings on Russia for Wilson has little to do with ideology but rather, as Professor Aaron pointed out, with the so-called Russian character—the oriental despotism to which the Russians are supposedly liable. This is the idea which fueled Richard Pipes's history of Russia, that Russian realities from the tsars through the general secretaries were the controlling, the dominating factor. What Wilson doesn't address, on his deathbed in 1972, as Solzhenitsyn would a year later in his preface when the *Gulag Archipelago* appeared in English, is the unique quality of Soviet despotism, Hannah Arendt's idea that this was based not, like the Nazis, on the technology of cruelty but rather on the mechanism of ideology, perfected in Stalin but appearing also in Lenin. Wilson failed to see this, as did others. My theme was the drama of dealing with one's own shifts, the difficulty of that, and my talk was not intended as a calling to accounts of a man whom I admire a great deal. That would be extremely arrogant of someone in my circumstances, who shows up in the Soviet Union in early 1988. The Soviet Union was just not as knowable in Wilson's time as it was when I was there. In fact Wilson did far better than most academics studying the Soviet Union. He went for five months and absorbed the experience of living in the same material conditions as many Russians. How many professors did that in the '30s?

Aaron: When Wilson was preparing to go to the Soviet Union, left-wing people, especially members of the Party, were very eager that he give a favorable report. In the *New Republic* there were certain people, Malcolm Cowley among others, who quickly made up their minds about the trials and remained apologists for the Stalinist regime for some time. Wilson didn't tip his mitt—he was very circumspect—but the letters he exchanged with John Dos Passos at this time reassured Dos Passos that he was not going to extenuate or defend the policies of the Communist Party. He would remain skeptical while keeping a more open mind than his friend. At this time the *New Republic* was hardly typical of the press in the United States, and the big press, most newspapers, were very hostile to the Left and looking for any kind of evidence to show that the Communists were villains and the enemy of the state. So it was between those two tendencies that Wilson assumed he had to steer.

Walzer: I would just note that parts of *To the Finland Station* were published in *Partisan Review* as well as in the *New Republic*, and also that *Partisan Review* had a very different political position at that time.

Aaron: I think one of the things that distinguished Wilson at this time from the partisans was that he was interested, as David Remnick says, in just getting information and the facts, so he talked to both sides when they were ostracizing each other and would not even cross the street if they were likely to meet the other person there. He maintained friendships with both Sidney Hook and Max Eastman, who was again one of his educators and from whom he learned a lot, although he certainly didn't agree with Eastman's views at the end, any more than he did with those of Dos Passos.

Paul Berman: Actually Sidney Hook's position in the '30s was not all that different from what you see with Edmund. In the middle of the book Wilson echoes the famous debate between Hook and Eastman in the mid-'30s on the nature of the dialectic. Both sides agreed on the general value of Marxism; the argument was really over what had gone wrong with it. And the complication in *To the Finland Station* is that Wilson finally

comes down on the side of Eastman, and it's the Eastman aspect of the book that explains the difference between David Remnick's and Michael Walzer's views of
Finland Station.

I think Walzer is entirely correct in saying that there
are very sharp premonitions throughout the book, un-
mistakable premonitions, that all this is not going to
work out well in the Soviet Union. At the same time,
however, there is this enormous enthusiasm for Lenin
at the Finland Station, and what explains this is Eastman's work. You have to remember that the American
intellectual who really devoted himself to Russia more
than anybody else was Eastman. He founded the
American tradition of defending the intelligentsia of
Russia with his book *Artists in Uniform* in 1934, the
tradition of defending the dissidents, writing from the
perspective of an admirer and friend of Trotsky. Eastman's theory was that Russia had indeed turned out
quite badly, but the fault, the reason that it had done
so, was the mystical element in Marx. It was not because of Lenin—Lenin was the good guy, Marx the
bad guy. This is an argument that underlies *To the Finland Station*. When you read the whole thing, you see
that Wilson is repeatedly saying this is not going to
work out but it's not Lenin who's to blame—Lenin is a
great man. I won't get into the Hook part. Suffice it to
say that all three of those men would have agreed on
the general progressive nature of the Russian Revolution; they would have agreed that things were now
turning out quite badly. And then they would have had
a philosophical argument over what the origins of the
bad aspects were.

Arthur Schlesinger: On the question of the *New Republic*, it must be remembered that Edmund Wilson broke with the magazine not over the Moscow Trials but over intervention versus isolation. He very much feared that England would drag the United States into another war. But he wasn't really a man of politics. He ignored the New Deal, didn't always vote, focused on literature and personality and society.

Remnick: But to turn Lenin into an author, and to see him almost solely as an author or artist instead of an architect of power, with incredible talent for grasping that power, is a great problem and a self-deception. Though I would agree that Wilson wasn't really political, that's itself a source of critical difficulty. I'm not willing to suppose, as some people do, that there is such a thing as immutable national character or that Russians are incapable of democracy. Russian history is full of complication and alternatives. There were complications, there were reformist elements—ask Vladimir Nabokov—there were all kinds of factions in the early twentieth century, and what won out was not a majority party but the most ruthless and effective player of power. This is not just a theoretical discussion. There's no question that theories propounded around the time of the Russian Revolution influenced social policy. That's a given. But on the question of power I find Wilson lacking in *To the Finland Station*.

Walzer: It is a matter of some interest that political journalists today, in dealing with the troubles of democracy in the New Russia, find themselves referring to and invoking the cultural traditions of both the Soviet Union and the Russia that preceded it.

Remnick: Sure, and there are certain clichés for it, and as a practicing journalist I know where they get started. For the last ten years, every year or so we've heard, for example, about the "time of troubles," because it is such a neat phrase to fit onto what have you—whether it's a bad harvest or Yeltsin's illness or Gorbachev's crisis. I'm not sure that these journalistic remarks, these journalistic stock phrases, come out of any great wellspring of knowledge about Russian or Soviet history.

Aaron: May I make one point clear? Do you say that Wilson was not interested in the subject of power?

Remnick: No, I just don't think he was expert at it in the way he was expert about God knows how many other things.

Aaron: Well, it's the whole question about the genesis of *To the Finland Station*. I don't think it started as a serious attempt to write a history of socialism. I think it had more to do with the sort of dramatic vision he had about how ideas take shape and the pleasure he took in seeing the various phases of this idea in the minds and practices of certain nineteenth-century socialists. He was interested in Utopianism, interested in the communistic experiments in the first half of the nineteenth century in this country. It was a pattern, a painting, a story that he was telling. He looked at it, I think, rather dispassionately. At least in *To the Finland Station* and *Travels in Two Democracies*, he wasn't so much concerned about some of the consequences that he had begun to hear about as he was with the grand picture.

Member of the Audience: David, in your talk you say that Wilson was at first jealous of Russian literary men. Can you clarify that?

Remnick: Well, who isn't? This is an old matter. I think it was difficult to live the life of a literary intellectual in the United States, struggling economically as Wilson did. He was not Edmund Wilson then. He went to Russia, as so many went to Eastern Europe and the Soviet Union before and long after, and in addition to being excited by the limitless political possibilities, he was at first impressed by the exalted place of Russian letters. American writers were still having this response until 1989, 1991. Some have been dazzled by the rewards of state sponsorship—I can't know what was in Wilson's mind. Much more recently, Philip Roth writes about going to Czechoslovakia that "in the East everything matters and nothing can be said," while here "everything can be said and nothing matters." For literary men, at least on vacation, that's an enviable state of affairs.

Member of the Audience: In reading *To the Finland Station* again I was reminded that what I like most about it has less to do with the station where it ended than with the many stations where the trip began. The first time I read the chapter on Michelet was actually the most striking—Wilson's combination of Vico and Michelet, trying to find a coherent Enlightenment tradition filtered through a nineteenth-century romanticism. That was one contribution of the book as an exercise in intellectual history. Now the train not only ended up at the station but went right through the station and crashed. I wonder if there is still some

stubbornness on Wilson's part to see the Enlightenment tradition as alive, if he's sticking by his faith that
somehow the human condition can be improved by the
exercise of reason, a democratic vision which the eighteenth century might not have produced as well as
Michelet could have?

Remnick: I think you're absolutely right. Jason Epstein made the point that the Enlightenment that created and so excited Wilson is the same Enlightenment
that disappointed figures like Nabokov and, more se-
verely and in a more eccentric way, Solzhenitsyn.

Aaron: I think the tension in *To the Finland Station*
and his other political writings is between the eighteenth-century idea of enlightenment and order, which
made him impatient with disorderly behavior in social
life and politics, and an impulse, on the other hand, to
sympathize with people who break away, who are romantic and lead messy lives. In Wilson's personal dealings with his friends he was torn. He was very sympathetic with those who didn't manage things very
well, and yet impatient with them at the same time.
This tension, which you can see in his letters, seems to
work into his writings and his response to politics.

Member of the Audience: One of the matters I'd like
discussed is Wilson's relationship with Nabokov.

Aaron: Well, I would say first that perhaps politics
did play some role, because Nabokov believed that
pre-1917 Russia was on its way to development and
progress. He thought the revolution interrupted democratic movements already in place, as well as the real
possibility of a parliamentary government. And this is a
position some Soviet historians take, believing that the

revolution was a disaster. I don't think Wilson could have brought himself to this point.

The actual story of the break between the two men is very complicated. But Wilson himself, I think, was rather bewildered by it. He hadn't counted on the rising level of acrimony. He said to me and some others that a playful quarrel, something of a hoax, had gotten out of hand. They were going to debate each other in the press and get things started, and then enjoy the resulting brouhaha, but for some reason what started out as friendly sparring ended in anger and recriminations. I think that Nabokov couldn't stand to be seen in public debating seriously with somebody who, from his point of view, knew so little about Russian language and literature. Then there were other issues—the fact that Wilson never liked *Lolita*, whereas Nabokov thought it one of his best books and expected a positive response from Wilson, who had encouraged Nabokov's career and praised his other work. So I think there was a whole series of reasons that prompted this discord.

Remnick: In their dispute about Russian I think Nabokov was mostly right. After all, his linguistic position was unassailable. Wilson had a decent, maybe better than a graduate student's, reading knowledge of Russian, but he couldn't speak a lick. It was unwise and a little vain of him to go on the way he did on certain points. However, unless you look at Nabokov's translation as a kind of absolutist trot, and the notes as a combination of scholarship and Borgesian humor—a kind of nonfiction *Pale Fire*—you have to admit that, read as a poem, his *Onegin* is terrible, and that, alas, was a point worth making. Incidentally, Wilson was far from the only one to make that point. As I remember reading about the dispute, Nabokov had been hit by Walter Arndt and a couple of others, and he was waiting for Wilson's review to come out in the *New York Review*, thinking there would at last be a friendly voice on his side, and he was deeply disappointed when there wasn't. So there were all sorts of personal angles to the dispute over *Onegin*, but as a translation it was eminently criticizable. If you give a student or a first-time reader of Pushkin the Nabokov translation, the person will likely hurl it through the window.

Aaron: What can you add about all this, Lewis?

Lewis Dabney: Their quarrel becomes sadder when you read the Wilson-Nabokov correspondence and see how remarkably generous Wilson was to Nabokov, who came here and had no clue how America worked. Wilson really took him by the hand. . . .

Remnick: I think he brought him to William Shawn's attention at the *New Yorker*.

Dabney: Wilson may have been jealous because *Lolita* did so much better than *Hecate County*, which had in some sense broken the way. He had so much wanted to be a novelist. But Dan is right that he never liked *Lolita*. After all, when it appeared he had a twelve-year-old daughter. His friend Helen Muchnic, whom he introduced to Nabokov and who had strong reservations about the man, observed to me that fathers of twelve-year-old girls are not necessarily going to like *Lolita*.

On the other subject, the translation of *Onegin*, Isaiah Berlin told me that he thoroughly agreed with Wilson's characterization of the translation as "perverse-pedantic-impossible." He wished, however, that Wilson had not rashly talked about Russian words he didn't fully understand.

Member of the Audience: Isn't it sad that literature is losing its special place in Russia?

Remnick: I don't think it's sad at all; I think it's normal. The great writers of the Soviet Union were imprisoned, and killed too, because they were alternative journalists. There was no honest journalism there of any kind, and yet certain writers were telling the "news," if they could manage to get it out, and so the reasons for their exalted positions were entirely perverse. There's a tradition of comments about this extraordinary position—Solzhenitsyn calls it a second government—but I think, thank God, that's all finished.

Aaron: If we're about to conclude, I'll tell an anecdote. I had a conversation with Wilson once about writers in the Communist Party in the '30s. He said that one thing that began to turn him off was when Waldo Frank said that when the Communists come to power everybody is going to be an intellectual: the president is going to be an intellectual, the vice president, all the way down to the postmaster general. For all his belief in ideas, it was that notion that horrified Wilson, that the intellectuals could be in control.

PATRIOTIC GORE AND THE INTRODUCTION

ARTHUR SCHLESINGER, JR.,
C. VANN WOODWARD,
AND OTHERS

Arthur Schlesinger: The discussion of *To the Finland Station* suggests that there were certain limitations in Edmund Wilson's reading of history. Nonetheless, he was absorbed by history as few men of letters are. We hear a lot of talk in literary circles about the new historicism. Well, Edmund Wilson was a practitioner of the old historicism. He was much influenced by Sainte-Beuve and by Taine, who once said, "Books do not fall from the sky like meteorites." Edmund Wilson understood the way in which literature emerges from the welter of confusion and contradiction that forms a historical context, and his absorption in history was a necessary condition to his understanding of literature.

Wilson was very proud of America, and therefore felt a sense of betrayal when American culture fell beneath the standards he expected of it. He was a patriot of a certain generation and style. Dan Aaron once asked him why he disliked the British so much, to which he answered: "Because of the American Revolution." Like the Adamses and Lodges of Massachusetts, he maintained a distrust of the British Empire left over from the War of Independence and the War of 1812, and his was perhaps the last generation who regarded the Revolution as still in some sense a contemporary event.

Other "old Americans" of the time were Charles A. Beard, Oswald Garrison Villard, William E. Borah, Amos Pinchot, Quincy Howe, Alice Roosevelt Longworth, Robert R. McCormick, even perhaps Norman Thomas; one can find traces of the tradition in younger men like George Kennan. These Americans disagreed vastly on most other issues, but they shared a revulsion against European wars, along with a marked strain of Anglophobia. They agreed with John Quincy Adams's exhortation to the young Republic: "Wherever the standard of freedom and independence has been or shall be unfurled, there will her heart, her benedictions, and her prayers be. But she goes not abroad in search of monsters to destroy." If America were to involve itself in all the wars "which assume the colors and usurp the standard of freedom . . . the fundamental maxims of her policy would insensibly change from *liberty* to *force*. . . . She might become the dictatress of the world. She would no longer be the ruler of her own spirit." Thus these twentieth-century nationalists felt betrayed when the Republic departed from hallowed practice to meddle in power politics abroad. As a second European war approached in the late '30s, they believed that—in the title of Quincy Howe's isolationist tract of 1937—"England Expects Every American to Do His Duty."

Wilson's inbred, robust isolationism, dating from his own experience in the war "to make the world safe for democracy," was strengthened by the belief, so indignantly expressed in the introduction to *Patriotic Gore*, that wars were a contemptible physiological necessity. It was strengthened, too, by the fact that he did not really have a political, far less a geopolitical, mind. "I find," he wrote about this time in his journal, "I am a man of the twenties. I am still expecting something exciting: drinks, animated conversation, gaiety, brilliant writing, uninhibited exchange of ideas." Literary intellectuals of the '20s were not notably interested in politics. The Depression forced politics upon the serious-minded, and Edmund succumbed. But workaday politics never engaged his full attention. After his fantasies about taking communism away from the communists and his ill-titled book about the United States and the Soviet Union, *Travels in Two Democracies*, he returned to the sort of commentary on literature, personality, and history that really engrossed him.

Patriotic Gore owes something to Wilson's response to twentieth-century American history, from World War I to Vietnam. The book finds him in intense, if at moments perplexing and even troubling, commitment to the crucial issues of the American past at the moment of the greatest threat to the American Union.

C. Vann Woodward: Wilson had worked on his Civil War subject for some fifteen years and had published

most of it in the form of essays in the *New Yorker*
and other places. He was a notoriously poor reader of
his own writing. He made the mistake of reading drafts
of many of these essays at a class he taught at Harvard,
boring his students to distraction and to dropping his
course in large numbers.

When he turned in the completed manuscript, he
told his Oxford editor, Sheldon Meyer, that he was sick
and tired of the book, and he confessed to Dan Aaron
that he got bored and depressed by it. Upon its publication in April 1962, one morning he woke up at 2:00
A.M. in a fit of mad violence and hurled his typewriter
across the room. He described it later as a paroxysm of
exasperation with his wife, Elena, combined with an
acute heart attack. She attributed it to the attempt to
drink himself out of a depression brought on by his
problems with the IRS and with numerous physical ailments. This fit of violence could hardly be explained by
the critical reception of his book, including a generous
review of my own.

Patriotic Gore is not a history of the Civil War and
was not intended to be one. It was instead essays on
twenty-seven figures from both North and South,
drawn in some fullness, with briefer reference to others. They are a selected group, not intended to be ex-
haustive. And his purpose is pretty clearly indicated by
his subtitle, *Studies in the Literature of the American
Civil War*. Note that preposition "in." He didn't say he
was covering the whole field, and he certainly did not.
The three major poets of the war period, Melville,
Whitman, and Dickinson, the latter of slight public importance, he thought, get only passing attention, and

three major novelists, Howells, Crane, and James, fare little better. Rather than professional men of letters—malingerers, as he called them—Wilson strongly preferred participants and combatants. In a letter he declared that their speeches, articles, diaries, letters, and minor works made the fiction about the war seem pale. As an editor and admirer of Mary Chestnut, I can only smile with pleasure at Wilson's reference to her brilliant journal, which he pronounced so much more imaginative and revealing than most of the fiction. Our understanding of what Robert Penn Warren called our Homeric war—without, of course, a Homer—would be the poorer without Wilson's contribution.

I should like to suggest two or three points that might be made the subject of general discussion. One such question is raised by Wilson's professed intention of writing amoral history. The main title he chose for the book, *Patriotic Gore*, seemed to dismiss with scorn all thought of idealism and heroism, glory, every line of the "Battle Hymn of the Republic," as well as all the heroic claims in the Confederate song from which he lifted his title. He would, he declared in the introduction, "remove the whole subject from the plane of morality," strip all participants of any pretension to moral superiority, and reveal the war as a competition for power for its own sake. He uses the figure of the sea slugs consuming each other to illustrate this point. Not only individuals but societies and institutions as well, including those for and against slavery, were subject to the same skepticism. The Civil War, like the cold war of his own time, he saw driven by blind lust for power, "not virtue but at bottom the irra-

tional instinct of an active power organism in the presence of another such organism."

While I admit that the historiography and the movie
and television interpretations of the American Civil
War are often awash with moralistic and heroic sentimentality, I am unwilling to deprive all the participants
of moral motivation and ignore the moral issues. Such
conflicts tormented many of the participants—right
against right, loyalty against duty, higher law against
constitutional law, home and community against state
and a nation, as well as brother against brother. Wilson
himself tacitly admits to such realities while struggling
for detachment from solemn myth and official cant.
How else could he have dealt in any credible way with
such figures as Harriet Beecher Stowe, Abraham Lincoln, Mary Chestnut, Oliver Wendell Holmes, and
Robert E. Lee? Wilson avoids moralizing, but he cannot avoid morals in that conflict.

More Wilsonian inconsistencies that might be explored in the discussion here are those involved in
maintaining his promise of neutrality as between North
and South. I find him harder on Yankee myths, leg-
ends, and self-righteousness than he proves to be on
their rebel counterparts. The explanation may be that
he has taken greater precaution against Union myths
to which he was more consciously vulnerable by birth
and breeding. Or it may be in part his visits to his Virginia cousins. He exhibits a curious indulgence at times
for Southern mythology. For example, he concedes
to Alexander Stephens the claim that the Southerners
have a very good case for regarding Northerners as
"treacherous aggressors," and he wonders "whether it

may not be true, as Stephens has said, that the cause of the South is the cause of us all." And goes on to remark, "There is in most of us an unreconstructed Southerner who will not accept domination, as well as a benevolent despot who wants to mold others for their own good."

I would welcome the views of my colleagues and those of you who have listened on any or all of these Wilsonian paradoxes.

Andrew Delbanco: Perhaps Sheldon Meyer can tell us a bit about how that introduction came to be. But I would echo what Michael Walzer was saying about *To the Finland Station*—that elements are detectable in the book which suggest it's a narrative that Wilson understood was moving toward catastrophe—and then we had a little argument about how highlighted they were compared with his romanticized portrait of Lenin. The elements that confirm the drift of the introduction are there in *Patriotic Gore*, particularly in the chapters on Grant and Sherman, for example, who are like sea slugs, up to a point a least. But there are other chapters which move into a completely different register where that notion of explaining human behavior drops away. So, I think it's dependent on his mood, in effect, how much he believed the thesis of the introduction. But I would love to hear from Mr. Meyer about the origins of the book.

Sheldon Meyer: *Patriotic Gore* took a long time in writing. It was conceived in 1947 as a study of nineteenth-century American literature from the Civil War through Edith Wharton. As the years passed, his concept changed. Meanwhile, I had inherited Wilson. This was an incredible event in my life, for Wilson had been

my personal literary hero ever since I had written my
senior thesis at Princeton. He was just about the only
left-leaning literary figure of the '30s who came out of
that period with his integrity and dignity intact.

When he finally brought the book in to me, now ex-
clusively on the literature of the Civil War, he had me
meet him at the Princeton Club. He stepped into the
bar with two huge binders containing the manuscript,
slumped in a booth, and promptly proceeded to down,
in turn, two double manhattans. He was talking in
more and more anxious and lugubrious terms about the
manuscript. He said he was sick and tired of it; it
needed to be cut, with its long quotations and accounts
of minor works, but he didn't have the inclination or
energy to do so. He then made a fervent appeal to me
for help: would I do the cutting of the manuscript for
him? I had doubts about the title and said to him, "My
God, why are you calling it that?" He replied, "No one
likes a dull title."

When I left the rather drunk Wilson, I was walking
on air. I had been given the chance to edit my literary
hero; I was going to be part of history, as Maxwell Perkins and some other famous editors had been. I would
be contributing in important ways to the publishing of
a classic (it indeed took me only a few pages of reading
to recognize that *Patriotic Gore* was such a classic). In
this challenged and exhilarated mood I slashed some
two hundred pages from the manuscript, sent the edited version back to Wilson, and anxiously awaited his
reponse. It quickly came. In his high-pitched, furious
voice he roared over the phone, "Meyer, you've ruined
it. Put back in everything you've taken out. The book is

fine as it is," and put down the receiver and subsequently wouldn't budge on cuts (though, as you may know, he later said he should have put the long De Forest chapter in an appendix). After the manhattans had worn off, he had obviously had second thoughts. I went back to being the fledgling editor I really was and banished all thoughts of becoming Maxwell Perkins.

Woodward: You've omitted your one victory over his resistance, Sheldon. May I tell it? He used the expression that a certain book had been "circling around this center for some time," and you quite rightly pointed out that you don't "circle around a center."

Meyer: I said that something either revolved around something or centered on something. He suddenly looked at me and said: "You know, you're right." I knew nothing about the introduction until it arrived on my desk.

Daniel Aaron: I still stick to my feeling that this introduction was not really an intrinsic part of the work. As I've suggested about Wilson's manner of composition, his way was to assemble his essays and reviews and create books from them. He added details that corroborated the ideas he had set forth in the introduction, in the interest of consistency. But my feeling is that when he was writing the reviews and then the chapters of *Patriotic Gore* he was not thinking of slugs and zoology. And I suspect that if you went back and looked at the original versions of the sections that ultimately make the book, you might find that passages had been added to complement the introduction. So I still think you could eliminate it and cut out those added details.

That wouldn't really change the quality of the book. I think it would improve it.

Arthur Schlesinger: May I comment? What Dan said makes me curious. Maybe Lewis knows—I mean, does the typescript survive? Is it possible to reconstruct the stages at which this book was written?

Lewis Dabney: I don't think what survives will resolve the issue. But let me tell a story in this connection. When I got acquainted with Wilson, shortly after *Patriotic Gore* appeared, I also knew Dan, who had told me that he and Stuart Hughes—then running for the Senate from Massachusetts as a peace candidate—had read a draft of the introduction. They went to upstate New York and tried to discourage Wilson from using it. *Life* magazine later editorially thundered against his grouping of Lincoln, Lenin, and Bismark. But Wilson enjoyed defying American chauvinists, and he wanted to be himself, which was one reason he resisted the advice of Dan and Stuart Hughes. Talking with him later, I said, "You know, it's possible they were right." Wilson's answer was, "I either had to take a lot out or put a lot more in, so I decided to put a lot more in."

Delbanco: On the attack on the rapacious central government in the introduction, in addition to Cuba, Vietnam, and all those international things, there was also the intervention in Little Rock, Arkansas. Did he mean to object to that?

Member of the Audience: That returns to what I think Vann Woodward was saying about why he seems to be stronger on the South than he does on the North.

There is this tic in Wilson, and it has to do with the lost cause, not in the moonlight-and-magnolias sense but in the sense that the South lost the first great battle against the leviathan state. And there is a tic in modern American letters, whether the writer goes right or left, in terms of attacking the leviathan state, seeing it as the great enemy. One of the greatest exemplars today is Gore Vidal, the last page of whose novel on Lincoln ends with what amounts to a summation of Edmund Wilson's introduction to *Patriotic Gore*. He likens Lincoln to Bismarck. A person who comes close to this now is Eugene Genovese, with a similar kind of rage against the leviathan state, no matter what its morals. Whether this state is intervening in Arkansas or taking away your tax money or whatever, it is the great abstract enemy. And that is something I think Wilson came to—it's not particular to him and I'm not sure when he came to it, but it's something that he helped start.

Schlesinger: I would like to file a dissent on that. Wilson was concerned about the imperialist state, but I don't think he was concerned about the social welfare state. After all, he voted for Norman Thomas most of his life. He was a strong supporter of John Kennedy and Robert Kennedy. He was wearing a McGovern button not long before he died. He did not believe that the state shouldn't intervene on behalf of the poor and helpless. I don't recall talking to him about Little Rock, but I'd be very surprised if he objected to what was done there. Though he had been rather indifferent to the New Deal at the time, I don't recall him expressing any anti-New Deal sentiments. He objected of course to FDR's foreign policy, and in domestic policy he later objected to the income tax, but that was a special, personal objection, and even in his income tax book it is stated in terms of foreign policy. He wasn't objecting to the income tax in principle, but to the fact that tax money was being used to finance a war of which he disapproved. He was not against the leviathan state in the sense that Newt Gingrich is. I don't think for a moment he would be in favor of turning federal responsibilities back to state and local government—he knew what state and local government was. But he was very much against the imperialist state.

Aaron: I agree with you. He hadn't liked Roosevelt personally. He spoke about his kind of creepy smile. But he was terribly glad when Roosevelt won his second election, simply because the people that he loathed were putting up such a holler. But I'd like to ask Vann a question about another Wilsonian paradox. There was a time when he was attacking Allen Tate and his friends among the Southern Agrarians, making fun of their notions of going back to an Old South and so forth. Yet, as you pointed out, he did have these southern cousins, and I was wondering if by the time he came to write *Patriotic Gore* these personal relationships had mitigated the heavy sarcasm in his letters to Tate and others, so that as he was writing the book he began to think of the South in a slightly different way than he did in the '30s?

Woodward: I don't find in *Patriotic Gore* any of the animosity that you call attention to. That may have been a passing conflict with personal acquaintances, and his later polemical views were the product of their time and place. But when he got down to writing seriously about Lincoln and Holmes and Robert E. Lee, it was a different story.

OMISSIONS IN

PATRIOTIC GORE

RANDALL KENNEDY,

TONI MORRISON,

AND OTHERS

Randall Kennedy: Preparing for this conference by reading and rereading work by Edmund Wilson has had a strongly deflationary effect on my estimation of his career. The thing that snagged my attention was a glaring absence of African-American writers in his discussion of American literary developments. In *The Shores of Light: A Literary Chronicle of the Twenties and Thirties* there is no mention of Jean Toomer or James Weldon Johnson or Claude McKay, Zora Neale Hurston or Langston Hughes or Sterling Brown—in other words, no suggestion of interest in the Harlem Renaissance. In *Classics and Commercials: A Literary Chronicle of the Forties* there is no mention of Richard Wright or Chester Himes. In *The Bit Between My Teeth: A Literary Chronicle of 1950 to 1965* there is no mention of Ralph Ellison or Lorraine Hansberry or Leroi Jones.

One of Wilson's claims to fame was the variety of his interests, the omnivorousness of his curiosity, the range of his reading. When it came to African-American literary culture, however, he mirrored the parochial, ethnocentric ignorance that characterized the literary establishment of his era.

In *The Bit Between My Teeth*, Wilson does devote two pages to James Baldwin. Wilson thought quite highly of Baldwin, and says the following in an interview:

> The only American fiction writers I always read are Salinger, James Baldwin, Edwin O'Connor. James Baldwin I think most remarkable. He is not only one of the best Negro writers that we have ever had in this country, he is one of the best writers that we have. He has mastered a taut and incisive style—which is what Negro writers often lack—and in writing about what it means to be a Negro he is writing about what it means to be a man. No one is more concerned with the Negro problem, and yet no one so far transcends it by intellect and style.

As far as I've been able to determine, however, Wilson nowhere elaborated upon his comments on Baldwin. Furthermore, although Wilson refers to other African-American writers in the course of praising Baldwin, one finds little or no reference to these writers in his criticism. This is striking, since Wilson turned so much of his reading into writing of various sorts. I find it odd, if not implausible, that he would have done such reading and not written about it.

In *Red, Black, Blond and Olive: Studies in Four Civilizations: Zuñi, Haiti, Soviet Russia, Israel*, published in 1956, Wilson discusses two West Indian authors. One whose work he briefly mentions is Dantes Bellegarde, described as "a very polished and upright old gentlemen, a mulatto, almost white." The other is Aimé Césaire, whose poetry Wilson praises as "the best thing of its kind—the symbolist prose poem which is also a dramatic monologue—since Rimbaud's *A Season in Hell*." According to Wilson, Césaire's poetry is "a brilliant performance which brings home the embittered role of the gifted and ambitious Negro contending against his difficult destiny with a force that seems as terrific as that of the acts and words of the heroes of the Haitian revolution." Wilson also briefly grapples with two Haitian writers. He says nothing about the race of Philippe Thoby-Marcelin and Pierre Marcelin but lauds their novels on the black Haitian peasantry, comparing them favorably to the novels of Ignazio Silone.

Whatever the race of Thoby-Marcelin and Marcelin, it is clear that, at least on occasion, Wilson was willing to recognize talent, genius, and heroism in a black skin. Hence, in addition to his praise of Baldwin and Césaire, he refers to Toussaint L'Ouverture as a great man deserving of a place beside those two other great liberators, Simón Bolívar and George Washington. Wilson, moreover, criticizes the race line in the United States as an undemocratic institution that deprives all persons, whites as well as blacks, of potentially instructive and enjoyable associations. "For a native of the

United States," he writes, "a trip to Haiti is immensely instructive. He may wonder whether segregation may not have kept him from knowing the best of American Negro life."

But then we confront one of the central books in the Edmund Wilson canon, *Patriotic Gore*, published in 1962, and see that the instructive lesson of the trip to Haiti has evidently failed to bear fruit. Subtitled *Studies in the Literature of the American Civil War*, *Patriotic Gore* gathers together and comments upon a broad tapestry of writings by such varied figures as Harriet Beecher Stowe, Abraham Lincoln, Ulysses S. Grant, William T. Sherman, Frederick Law Olmsted, Colonel Wentworth Higginson, Mary Chestnut, Robert E. Lee, George Fitzhugh, Hinton Helper, Alexander Stephens, and so on.

Virtually absent from *Patriotic Gore*, in what must rank as one of the most egregious oversights in the history of literary studies, is the voice of the slave, the fugitive slave, or the free Negro. Absent from *Patriotic Gore* is any mention of Sojourner Truth, Harriet Jacobs, or William Wells Brown, all of whom had produced fascinating memoirs about their enslavement and freedom. Wilson even manages to omit Frederick Douglass from his discussion of the literature of the Civil War, despite Douglass's many extraordinary speeches and three remarkable autobiographies. Orlando Paterson aptly described Frederick Douglass as perhaps the most eloquent slave in world history. Yet Wilson somehow managed to overlook him.

Wilson does bring in the experience of Charlotte Forten, a free black woman from the North who, after the Civil War, journeyed south to educate former slaves. But the brief, desultory examination of Forten in *Patriotic Gore* only accentuates the omission of Douglass. Charlotte Forten, after all, was no Frederick Douglass.

These stark and unjustifiable omissions raise questions about Wilson's basic competence as a literary historian. It makes one consider more sympathetically Stanley Edgar Hyman's withering but accurate observation that Wilson may have been at his best as merely "an introductory critic" whose "value decreases in direct proportion to the literacy of his audience and its familiarity with the work he is discussing." Louis Rubin and Perry Miller made similar criticisms. Miller, for example, said of *Patriotic Gore* that Wilson "assumes a tone such as one might use had he never heard of these authors before. Considering the vast amount of scholarship that has been devoted to Mrs. Chestnut, let alone Grant, Sherman or Hinton Helper, Mr. Wilson's pronouncements generally emerge as fulminations about the familiar."

The overconfident ignorance that may have led Wilson to fulminate about familiar white writers also allowed him to leave in the shadows unfamiliar black ones. This represents a major intellectual failing—a failure to know one's subject. And it makes me question whether there are other, similar, failings in the large Wilson oeuvre that await the unwary reader.

I'd like to conclude by taking up a point that has been made in comparisons of literary journalists to academic specialists. Reading Wilson has made me more appreciative of academic qualities which are often minimized. In some of the commentary on Wilson—I think, for instance, of a piece by Alfred Kazin comparing Wilson to academics—he is said to be wide-ranging and without a sense of defensive propriety about intellectual turf. I must say, though, that in reading Wilson I have gained new respect for the academic's demand for thoroughness, punctiliousness with respect to giving intellectual credit, and, indeed, modesty. I'm more appreciative of academics who, declining to attempt to master everything, do master their subject when they present a book to the public.

I hope that my comments have not been churlish. I offer them against a backdrop of opinion that has often presented Edmund Wilson as an exemplary critic. He was not.

David Bromwich: It seems to me, in thinking about critics, good to use the same principle of charity in interpretation that we try to use about authors, and even about each other. Critics ought to be judged by the usual intelligence and the exceptional intelligence that they show in what they do talk about.

The Harlem Renaissance, which is in the front of everybody's mind now, and rightly so as a major event in American culture, wasn't in that same place in people's consciousness in the '30s, the '40s, or even the '60s. That was true of a great many writers, including writers who were much more avowedly and articulately free of racial prejudice than Edmund Wilson.

I'd be very interested to know what Randall Kennedy thinks of *Patriotic Gore*, and what's in it, not what's not in it, rather than what Perry Miller thinks, because his lengthy remarks could have been made without reading the book—though I'm sure he has read it. One of the canons of the intellectual propriety to which he appeals against Wilson is that you ought not merely to comment upon the book but to address its substance in some way.

Kennedy: I'll put aside the last comment. With respect to charity of interpretation, it would be one thing if people said, here's a guy who wrote an awful lot and made a contribution. That's not what people say, though. People in our own time speak about Edmund Wilson and don't have anything as far as I can see to say that's critical whatsoever. They speak of Edmund Wilson as the great American man of letters. But he also has a major deficiency with which we should be concerned, and which may not make him exemplary. Now what's uncharitable about saying that?

Ann Hulbert: I don't see how you can say we have been uncritical of Wilson. With all that has been said about him today, the notion that exemplary could possibly mean without flaws seems odd. Wilson has been criticized for sometimes overly relying on general ideas, while being more truly interested in individual writers and historical figures. We've heard people say that he didn't read poetry very well. But we've also been trying to understand his unique role, to try to comprehend all he did and how he did it.

Jed Perl: For me, *Patriotic Gore* is a work of art, and as such is extraordinarily compelling. It has a density, a way of going into people's lives, seeing people coping with their lives, day by day, all kinds of very specific

tiny things in the lives of all kinds of people, and to ask
for what is not within its limits as a work of imaginative
literature, I think, is to deny the possibility of imaginative literature. The issue is not racism, or one or another view of what the Civil War was about. Within
that book's specific conventions the shape of the book
is totally convincing. I think it's fair to compare Wilson
with Parkman, to say that Francis Parkman's history of
the French and Indian Wars and *Patriotic Gore* are the
two greatest works produced about the cultural experience of this country. To accuse the book of racism not
on the basis of what is included there, but on the basis
of what is not, is to me perverse.

Daniel Aaron: When we ask why Frederick Douglass
is not there, I think this has something to do with the
way this book was put together and so many of his
other books were put together. He didn't start out to
write a history of American writing about the Civil
War—and this touches on what has been said earlier
about how he made a living as a literary journalist. He
would review books on American authors and then assemble the pieces very artfully. The bulk of *Patriotic
Gore*—I'd have to check with Lewis Dabney about
this—but I believe that almost the whole book was
based on these articles. No book on Frederick
Douglass came out during the '50s, which says something about the limited racial awareness of the whole
culture. If there had been, I think Wilson might very
well have written about him, and written about him
generously.

Kennedy: If you want to redefine the book in the way
that you've suggested, that's fine. If you want to say, it's

not really a book of history, it's not really covering the
whole literature of the Civil War, it's a man writing
about books that happened to come out during a particular period of time that he happened to put together—
if that's what you want to say, then that's one thing. But
of course that's not the way the book has been handed
down to us. That wasn't the meaning behind the statement made by a very distinguished person here: "No
single work goes deeper into the meaning and the implications of the Civil War experience for its more articulate participants." Now that evaluation by C. Vann
Woodward seems to have in mind more than the sort of
journalistic work Mr. Aaron is talking about, one that
has a breadth and a solidity to it. That's the view of *Patriotic Gore* that I'm questioning. Now if you want to
narrow the book and make it less than that, well, that's
a different kettle of fish.

To get back to the question that was asked a while
ago about what I think of *Patriotic Gore*, he made a
lot of interesting points and quotable statements about
a variety of people and developments. But in reading
Patriotic Gore again—it was a rereading—I was struck
by what seemed to be a certain lack of knowledge.
One of the people I'm most interested in, perhaps
because he's a lawyer, is Albion Tourgée. There are interesting things about Tourgée, this guy who goes
south and fights on the side of the Reconstructionist
regimes and then writes these novels which sympathize with the Southerners whom Tourgée was fighting
against. But there's no reference to the later part of
Tourgée's life in which Tourgée is the lawyer, in 1896,
for Homer Plessy in *Plessy v. Ferguson*. And the only

reason I state that is my hope that a person delivering
a book of this sort would know the subject thoroughly.
I got the sense that this wasn't a thorough book, a
knowledgeable book. I'm making a claim against the
literary-cultural-social-critical knowledge competence
of Edmund Wilson, and I still make it, and I would say,
the discussion of Tourgée shows it. Not that he didn't
make useful points—he did—but does this work merit
the sort of commentary that surrounds it? In my view
it's not very useful.

Toni Morrison in the Audience: An unease has crept
into this gathering at the intrusion of race and the possibility of racism into our discussion about Edmund
Wilson. I want to say that something in Randall Kennedy's talk made me uncomfortable also, and I want to
explain the source of that discomfort. First of all, having read some of Wilson's notebooks and diaries, I
think that any comments he might have chosen to make
on Frederick Douglass or certain other African-American writers or figures would have been of almost no
use. The suggestion that he admired Harriet Beecher
Stowe's ability to enter into the minds of black people
so successfully [a point that had been made from the
audience] seals my view. I am very happy that Wilson
chose to be brilliant about what he did know, and I
have always admired him for that.

The second part of my comment, the source of my
real unease—and I apologize for making it personal,
but I do think about these things in a personal way—is
associated with Edmund Wilson's position as the grand
man of letters, the man of American letters. Some

would say the grand white man of letters, and that would take care of that. But for the first ten years of my own writing life there was constant and persistent criticism of my fiction because it did not include any white people as major characters. I would be very upset if I believed that fifty years from now anybody who was still interested in my work condemned it because I had chosen to write principally about African-Americans' life experience, language, etcetera. I would not like it if they assumed from this that I was incapable of understanding or revealing or knowing anything about white Americans.

Part of what you say, Randall, has its obvious point. But on the other hand, it is the ideal for an intellectual or a writer, a man or woman of letters, to do what he or she wishes without having always to be inclusive. There are many, many things that Edmund Wilson didn't write, and many things that he did. And I would hate to have that burden of inclusiveness on me after fifty or a hundred years.

Kennedy: You have to be selective—that's what I said earlier. The world's a big place and he wrote about all sorts of things. But if you wrote a book about literary America in 1994, let's say, by Toni Morrison—

Morrison: Let's say, 1934—

Kennedy: So you wrote a literary book about 1934, I don't care, whichever year, but if anybody wrote a book about literary America today or literary America in the '40s, if that's the name of your book, then write about literary America in the '40s. If you decide to write a different sort of book I wouldn't have a squawk. Or if people weren't making these claims for Wilson I wouldn't have a squawk. Why I squawk is he writes a book with the title *Studies in the Literature of the Civil War* and leaves out a big hunk. If you do that, it seems to me there's a problem. He didn't have to name the book what he named it.

A GREAT MAN'S
LIMITATIONS

DAVID BRADLEY

As a young person who took ideas seriously yet had all the emotional immaturity which youth suggests, I was angered by a need to wonder, hurt personally by the facts of intellectual life, from a black perspective. But eventually I came to feel a sort of sorrow. Not sorrow at what this meant to me, but sorrow at what this ultimately meant for the major American thinkers and writers who could not speak to me. For to extend James Baldwin's metaphor, what does the parent lose by ignoring a child, even if that child is a bastard? What does a thinker lose by ignoring the evidence history has put before him or her? I felt sorrow at the thought that, great as these men were, they could have been greater, and I richer.

Edmund Wilson was—let me say this clearly—a courageous individual who could and would go into any area that took his interest, master it, and say something significant about it. If he was a public intellectual, he was also an intellectual treasure. Although of course

he said most about literature, in both a contemporary
and a historical sense, he said a lot about a lot of
things—history, of course, and the Iroquois, and the
Dead Sea Scrolls, and Haiti. And he said them for a
long time. Wilson was an acute and accurate observer,
a brilliant thinker and precise writer, and a brave traveler in every sense of the word. He aspired, I believe,
to be what Henry James called for—a person on whom
nothing was lost. Indeed, this was one of his deepest
ambitions. And, to a great extent, he achieved that ambition. He saw a lot, and saw it clearly, said a lot, and
said it brilliantly, and in so doing said a lot about American thought, and American thinkers.

There were things that Edmund Wilson seems not to
have seen, things he perhaps found somehow unspeak-
able, and surely left unspoken. At the risk of being re-
petitive, I remind you of some of the more salient. In so
doing I hope I do not appear ungracious—but our
America has not much of a history of graciousness, and
when one speaks of things historical, one can only be so
gracious and still tell the truth. Wilson seems to have
missed the Harlem Renaissance, which was surely the
most exciting and central artistic event of the '20s. It
has been pointed out that he does, in fact, refer to Jean
Toomer in *The Shores of Light*. Never mind that Jean
Toomer had nothing much to do with Harlem—indeed, was involved with the downtown crowd and
Wilson's associates Boni and Liveright and Waldo
Frank. But that one line means that Wilson was not unaware. He was in some kind of denial.

Well, some would say, that was the '20s, that things
were different then. Indeed they were. The Ku Klux

Klan had a summer camp in New Jersey, not too far from Wilson's hometown. Wilson knew it, for he wrote from Red Bank in 1925:

> I have attempted to divert the monotony of my existence in the country by inviting members of my family and old friends of my youth to dinner. A good deal of scotch makes this possible, and even rather interesting—I have adopted a policy of making them drunk and provoking them to reveal themselves. Last night, I had with her husband a girl on whom I had a great crush when I was a boy, and whom I have not seen for it must be more than fifteen years. . . . In the course of conversation, it appeared that she and her husband were enthusiastic supporters (though not actual members) of the Ku Klux Klan and believed that it had saved the country in preventing Al Smith from becoming President—they think neither Catholics nor Jews are "Americans." The Klan has a great hold on New Jersey.

The Ku Klux Klan in fact had a great hold on much of the country. The Ku Klux Klan was lynching people and terrorizing people. And yes, some of those people were Jews and Catholics. But don't you find it just a little odd that even in the context of the Ku Klux Klan, Edmund Wilson did not mention blacks?

Wilson had a certain degree of power. And it is therefore obvious that, in 1925, when Alain Locke put together an issue of *Survey Graphic*, and later the book *The New Negro*, which, Locke said, "aims to document the transformations of the innner and outer life of the

Negro in America that have so significantly taken place in the last few years," he was making an appeal for the attention of men like Wilson. He got attention from some men like Wilson—men like Waldo Frank and Carl Van Vechten. But Locke did not get attention from Wilson. A lot of people didn't, I should add. In January 1924, when he wrote to John Peale Bishop that "Mary is going to be in O'Neill's new play, which is about a white woman who marries a Negro—Mary is going to be the white woman and we are both expecting to be assassinated by the Ku Klux Klan," he for some reason did not add that the Negro was to be acted by Paul Robeson. Edmund Wilson seemed to be uninterested.

In *To the Finland Station* Wilson wrote—and it seems to me to be the heart of Wilson's greatness: "But one cannot enter into human history once it has taken place; nor can a man of the nineteenth century really recover the mentality of the sixteenth. One cannot reproduce the whole of history and yet keep the forms and proportions of art. One cannot care so much about what has happened in the past and not care what is happening in one's own time. One cannot care about what is happening in one's own time without wanting to do something about it." This statement, I would argue, suggests a rather more complicated reading of *Patriotic Gore*. It has been asserted that Wilson had all sorts of reasons for whom he picked, and whom he did not pick to write of there. In the introduction Wilson notes that, as the '60s dawned in the South, the Negroes were "rebelling against the whites, who are afraid of them, as they have always been, and do not want them to better themselves because they do not want to have to compete with them," while the whites were rebelling against what they saw as an oppressive federal government. He continues: "It is possible to sympathize with both Negroes and whites though not with the hoodlum and criminal methods employed by the latter against desegregation, which have left the Negro leaders with their non-violent methods in a position of moral superiority." But in the book itself, the effect of Wilson's selection from the literature of the Civil War was to follow only one branch of his own logic; if indeed it was possible to sympathize with both Negroes and Southern whites, why did the book fail so thoroughly to explore the place of black Americans in history, as were such white scholars as Herbert Aptheker and Kenneth Stammp? In this context *Patriotic Gore* looms large as an opportunity, and larger as an opportunity lost.

Lost in one sense because Wilson accepted the line of Frederick Jackson Turner of the unimportance of slavery as a cause of the war. But lost also because he did not look at history through what was beginning to happen around him. The obvious candidate for inclusion would have been Frederick Douglass. But perhaps a more intriguing candidate, especially in light of Wilson's penchant for the noncanonical writer, is Elizabeth Keckley, whose autobiography, *Behind the Scenes: Thirty Years a Slave and Four Years in the White House*, was published in 1868 and republished in 1931. However, we're told that what Wilson included in *Patriotic Gore* were almost entirely the books which passed across the literary horizon through the '50s, while he was writing it. Another interesting candidate, given Wilson's sea slug metaphor, would have been George Washington Williams, who was born in my hometown, Bedford, Pennsylvania. In 1863, while still a boy, he ran away and enlisted in the Union Army, was wounded and mustered out, but then reenlisted and served in Texas under General N. J. Jackson. When the Civil War was over, he enlisted in the army of Benito Juarez. Later, he was appointed as minister to Haiti—which suggests a reason why Wilson, given his passion for background, should have been aware of him. We should see these figures, or figures like them, in *Patriotic Gore*. Indeed, what is gorier than slavery?

Edmund Wilson makes me sad not because of what he failed to do but because he seems to have often felt alone, even when there were men and women who shared his beliefs and sentiments. There was culture that he did not see, that he might well have enjoyed. There were men like W. E. B. Du Bois, who was either at once or serially, historian, a sociologist, an essayist, who, just a few years before Wilson entered Princeton, had taken up residence in New York as director of information for the National Association for the Advancement of Colored People, and who stayed there through the '30s. What might Wilson have done had he spoken to Du Bois, the socialist who was tried for the crime of advocating world peace? What, indeed, might he have done if Du Bois had been teaching at Princeton when Wilson matriculated?

What is Wilson's place in history? He was born into the era of *Plessy v. Ferguson*. He saw the advent of *Brown v. Board of Education*—and he, self-confessedly, could not keep up. He was a man of the American times, and it is not his fault if they were not the best of times. But it is somewhat his fault that our times are not better than they are. He is a man who was searching for something among all the tribes save one. He was a man with tremendous intellectual reach but also a man whose intellectual reach not only exceeded his ability to grasp and his willingness to grapple but was shortened by his personal inabilities. Some may find that ungenerous. But as a black American, I have had to learn to see all the really great figures of our history as double figures. Indeed, this is what black Americans—and I would argue, all Americans—must do with American history itself if we are not to go mad, something, I would also argue, Wilson never quite figured out how to do. And so his reality was wanting. But his ideal was not.

It is important that we judge him as a man not of our times but of his own times, and not by our ideals but by his. For, as he wrote, a man of the nineteenth century cannot really recover the sixteenth. It is by his ideals, then, that I find his reality wanting: "One cannot care so much about what has happened in the past and not care what is happening in one's own time. One cannot care about what is happening in one's own time without wanting to do something about it." I believe Wilson wanted to do something about it. I believe he simply did not see how he could.

WILSON DIVIDED

ANDREW DELBANCO

I AM STARTLED by reading Edmund Wilson. When I
think about why, I recall an experience I had twenty-
five years ago when I had the chance to hear—or, more
accurately, to overhear—Rudolf Serkin rehearse the
Beethoven Choral Fantasy before a public concert.
There was in Serkin's playing a commitment to the
music utterly uncompromised by the preliminary nature of the occasion; he played with a fervor indistinguishable from what he brought a few hours later to the
public performance. Reading Wilson recalls for me this
experience of overhearing a great artist give expression
to a private passion.

Wilson had the capacity to be surprised by his own
delight. He is the kind of reader one strives to be: he
does not simply work within the boundaries of an already established structure of thought and feeling but
turns literary experience into new ideas and new sensations. This gift for what might be called revising himself
is particularly evident when he turns to writers who
were previously known to him only through a haze of

secondhand associations. "To expose oneself in maturity to *Uncle Tom*," as he puts it in *Patriotic Gore*, "may therefore prove a startling experience."

In Wilson's own writing there is a peculiar combination of belligerence and enthusiasm, a voice that's somehow sophisticated and callow at the same time. We have, I think, no problem hearing the sophistication; it's the other side, the not-quite-repressible believer, that I want to try to amplify.

In what did Edmund Wilson believe? He was clear about what he did not believe. He did not believe in sentimentality or melodrama, and he had no patience with euphemism and circumvention, with any kind of fancy talk. This preference for directness has something to do with the rather clinical passages about sex that one finds in the journals. He didn't want sex dressed up in the finery of love, just as he didn't want war dressed up in the rhetoric of high purposes. But if it was evasion that he stood against, to what was he positively committed? If he really believed the account he gives in the infamous introduction to *Patriotic Gore* of man as nothing better than a carnivorous sea slug, how could he have devoted his life to studying man's artistic productions? What was the relation in his mind between the imagination and the sheer animal rapacity of man?

One place to seek an answer is in the beautiful essay on John Jay Chapman, one of the most moving pieces Wilson wrote. The Chapman essay marks an exception to David Bromwich's observation that Wilson's style is almost "without heights." Wilson's study ends with a stunning metaphor that he quotes from Chapman on his deathbed—his request to his wife that she should "take away the mute. . . . I want to play on the open strings." One of Wilson's internal contradictions is revealed here. He identifies himself as a writer "fundamentally unsympathetic with all modern manifestations of religion," yet approves of Chapman's reservations about pragmatism, as expressed in a remarkable letter to William James. "I have a notion," Chapman wrote to James, "that I could tell you what's the matter with pragmatism if you'd only stand still. A thing is not truth till it is so strongly believed in that the believer is convinced that its existence does not depend on him. This cuts off the pragmatist from knowing what truth is." We hear again Wilson the seeker when he quotes another of Chapman's remarks: "There's only one real joy in life, the casting at the world the stone of an unknown world." These phrases confirm the accuracy and intelligence of what Jason Epstein and Mark Krupnick have said about Wilson's attachment to the Jews, and to the kind of Hebraic Protestantism that in the American tradition we call Puritanism. Jason said that these people had "placed beyond human reach the caretaker of their own standards." Such a vision, or the hope of retrieving it, seems to me to have animated Wilson throughout his lifetime.

For this reason, *Patriotic Gore* is one of our great jeremiads. Before he contemplated the possibility that belief had been lost somewhere in the irretrievable past, Wilson had made an effort through Marxism to recover it for himself. The chief literary result of this

effort was the book he published in 1940, *To the Finland Station*. But Marxism, for Wilson as for so many
others, did not endure as an object of belief. By 1953,
when he published the first version of his essay on
Lincoln, and in the later expanded version published in
Patriotic Gore, Wilson becomes hostile to the idea that
history manifests a divine will that somehow takes possession of men and works out its intentions through
them. This idea, he says, "is most familiar today as one
of the characteristic features of Marxism, in which it
has become the object of a semireligious cult and has
ended by supplying the basis for a fanaticism almost
Mohammedan."

There's a hint here that for Wilson the quest for
belief inevitably devolves into a kind of Manichean fanaticism. This devolution is a recurrent theme in his
work, even in his fiction, as in the story "The Man Who
Shot Snapping Turtles," about a man who becomes
convinced that the war between the mallard ducks and
the turtles in his backyard pond is a microcosm of the
grand cosmic war between good and evil. If this story
verges on satire, it is saved from the spirit of disdain
because Wilson both pities and loves the man.

It is in this sense that Wilson's work may be thought
of as an extended jeremiad, an account of how religious
belief is inevitably deflected into zealotry or nationalist
mania or some other destructive insanity. The Chapman essay takes as its theme the decay of the religious
impulse. "Truly," he quotes from one of Chapman's letters (speaking, I think, for himself), "it is the decay in
the American brain that's the real danger. And in my

narrow philosophy, I see the only cure in self-expression, passion, feeling, spiritual reality of some sort."

Wilson is writing about the same decay when he turns to the failure of sexual energy in the story "Ellen Terhune," his veiled account of Edna Millay. Here is the moment in the story when the narrator comes to visit Ellen, who is a musician and a composer. He listens as she performs one of her own pieces:

> This piece, which she said was the second movement, began with a four-note theme that sounded simple and conventional enough, and I was prepared for something genuinely classic; but the theme was not given the development one expects in the sonata form, nor did it even get the kind of variation that one finds in a passacaglia. She did not even retard or speed it up: she simply played it over and over. It was as if she did not know what to do with it, and the listener was constantly subjected to the embarrassment of fearing that the pianist had got stuck like a phonograph which stutters. There was at moments a suggestion of a second theme that seemed to play about the first in a flimsy and trivial manner, but this would fade off in atmospheric chords and leave the field to the original four notes, as boring and inexpressive as ever. It was like a perverse child, compelled to practice on a summer day, and deliberately annoying the household. At the end, the ghost of a second theme limped off and dropped away in irremediable speciousness and impotence, and we

were back with the same confounded phrase,
which was never satisfactorily resolved, but simply
repeated eight times at precisely the same loud-
ness and tempo.

A story about what we could call today dysfunction
(here expressed through a metaphor that links music
with sex), "Ellen Terhune" bears a resemblance to
Wilson's larger narrative of American history in *Patriotic Gore*—which, like any account of breakdown or
decline or obstruction, posits a lost moment of coherence or integrity. In the world of "Ellen Terhune," that
moment is evoked in a compressed backward glance
to the time of Ellen's father: "Those tragedies of the
turn of the century, I thought. It was one thing to die
or be broken for a political ideal or a social order as
had happened to both Southerners and Northerners in
the years of the Civil War, but to die, to be crushed,
to be shattered through the overpowering progress of
big business, through the unrestrained greed of specu-
lation, seemed hard on those men and women whom
we remember as gentle and bright and who look at us
in such photographs as those which Ellen produced
from a drawer, with the American friendliness and candor." This golden moment in the past was lost somewhere before the advent of the great state apparatus,
the combinations, the trusts, and those contemporary
bureaucratic entities that Wilson loathed and to which
he assigned initials such as IRS and MLA. In the bitter
introduction to *Patriotic Gore*, the culprits are the biggest conglomerates of all, the United States and the

USSR, which Wilson finds indistinguishable in their mindless enmity.

But in the actual narrative of *Patriotic Gore* the sense of loss is much more diffused and scattered, as befits the scale of the book and the fact that it was written over a period of years. Still, the same tragic theme of spent passion is implicit in the chapter on the "chastening of American prose style," where Wilson writes with impatience about the clotted passages of *Billy Budd*, which, he says, make it "one of the most inappropriate works for reading in bed at night, since it's easy to lose consciousness in the middle of one." It would seem that Wilson welcomes the realists such as Howells and Crane, who broke up the "close-knit blocks" of prose in Melville's *Moby Dick* and ventilated their prose style until it became transparent to the social reality they wanted to disclose. It would seem that Wilson was bidding good riddance to the old prose poets like Melville, and was relieved to arrive at the machine-age prose that he identifies particularly with John W. De Forest. In fact, I believe he was secretly mourning what had been lost in this succession, as when he says of Ambrose Bierce, one of the practitioners of the new style of naked description, that "some short circuit had blown out an emotional fuse in him."

Patriotic Gore is a book about people who try to keep the current going. Stowe, Grant, Julia Ward Howe, even Lincoln himself, are, Wilson thinks, all in the grip of a delusion—but it is a delusion the critic is desperate not to give up. For Stowe it is the idea that "every worthy person in the United States must desire to preserve the integrity of our unprecedented Republic." The irony is that this idea of a continually reconsecrated truth is precisely what gives the literature of the war on both sides, North and South, its tragic power. The tragedy is that the truth turns out to be an idea in collision with itself: in the South it means states' rights and human property rights; in the North it means a Union built on free labor.

The book, in fact, is divided against itself. In opposition to the long account of how Americans fell into the convulsion of civil war, we have the brief introduction, where Wilson makes his case that this war was the crisis from which America emerged as an engorging imperial monster, one of those nation-state sea slugs that opens its body to swallow up smaller creatures in a meaningless cycle of consuming. The war has nothing to do with principles or beliefs. In this view, it is part of a natural process more like ingestion and excretion than thinking. Despite the tacked-on quality of this introduction, there are traces of it in the narrative itself through which the whole of *Patriotic Gore* echoes its theme, as, for instance, when Wilson shows us General Sherman's "growing appetite for warfare" and credits him with inventing what the Germans would perfect in his own century as *Schrechlichkeit* in World War I and blitzkrieg in World War II.

This is a portrait of America as a nineteenth-century version of the expansive nation-state that emerged in the twentieth century, not only in the instance of the United States. In this sense, as Paul Berman has noted in his essay on Wilson in the *New Republic*, the South is the hero of *Patriotic Gore* if only because it is the region that stands against the future monster. In

"The Scout Toward Aldie," Melville's poem about the pursuit by Union forces of the Confederate guerilla John Mosby, Wilson sees Mosby as a warrior fighting not just against the Union army but against Union presumption. Mosby fights on behalf of a South that seeks to check the Northern apocalyptic fervor for what Alexander Stevens (whom Wilson quotes with approval) called "the demon of centralism, absolutism, despotism."

And yet the paradox that makes *Patriotic Gore* a great book, despite its lapses into tirade and invective, is Wilson's recognition that out of the Northern mania and the Southern response came a body of exquisite writing that he puts beside the writings that F. O. Matthiessen (another critic who wrote in the spirit of unrequited belief) had earlier named the "American Renaissance." Wilson's recurrent theme is that art is the companion of barbarism. Berman observes that *Patriotic Gore* can be thought of as an upside-down version of *To the Finland Station*, but I would suggest that it is also a rewriting of *The Wound and the Bow*. It is a book about the intimate relation between pain and creation.

For Wilson, this relation was the imprisoning paradox of human experience, which, in *Patriotic Gore*, he happens to evoke in the form of an American historical narrative. His theme is how the most passionate of human impulses—religion in *Patriotic Gore*, sex in some of the fiction—tend to be deflected and distorted into other channels of expression. By one kind of transformation, they become art, which was the obsessive subject of Wilson's study, and the object of his love. By another kind of transformation, they become politics or technology or war, which were the objects of his hatred and rage.

What made Wilson a major writer in the elegiac mode was his recognition that these impulses toward creation and destruction were linked in a kind of perpetual dance, like the fratricidal North and South of *Patriotic Gore*. Despite its elisions and distortions, *Patriotic Gore* is a great book because, through its portraits of Grant and Lincoln and Sherman and the rest, it tells a story about the simultaneous human aspiration for transcendence and the descent into vengence and violence. It is because *Patriotic Gore* is a book in which the tensions are vibrant and as of yet unresolved, because they are grounded in the human condition, that it will continue to be read.

PERSPECTIVES

EDMUND WILSON

IN HIS TIMES

LOUIS MENAND

EDMUND WILSON is a name that comes up whenever people start lamenting the disappearance of something called the public intellectual. The association is too simple, for two reasons. One is that if a public intellectual is a person who volunteers to reflect in print on the poverty of our common condition, the United States today is certainly not lacking for them. The other reason is that Wilson's relation in his own lifetime to this abstraction, "the public intellectual," was much more ambivalent than the way it is usually represented.

Wilson is sometimes grouped, in anthologies and histories of criticism, with the New York intellectuals. This is misleading, in part because Wilson had relatively little contact, apart from that consequential to his brief marriage to Mary McCarthy, with the New York intellectuals, but more importantly because Wilson belonged to an older generation and identified with it all his life. Wilson thought of himself as a man of the nine-teenth century (when he was feeling especially cur-

mudgeonly, he liked to talk about himself as a man of
the eighteenth century), and he always regarded his
generation as the generation of the '20s, not, as was the
case for most of the New York intellectuals, of the '30s.

Belonging to this senior generation exposed Wilson
to two events that younger intellectuals could not have
experienced firsthand. One was the First World War,
the other the modernist revolution in literature. Wilson
was a preppie. He attended the Hill School and then
Princeton, where he came under the influence of
Christian Gauss, for whom he maintained a filial respect all his life and to whom he dedicated *Axel's Castle*
in 1931. It is easy, because of that dedication, to imagine Gauss as a high modernist. But he was not. He was
a man of the 1890s who had known Wilde, who held
the English Victorians in disdain, and who regarded
Flaubert as the great literary master by virtue of his
aestheticism. This aestheticism, and a certain gentility,
is evident in some of Wilson's undergraduate contributions to the campus literary journal, the *Nassau Literary Magazine*, and it is hard to recognize in them the
enthusiastic reviewer of *Ulysses* and *The Waste Land*
only a few years later.

The war discouraged the gentility and encouraged
the sense of social engagement which was also part of
Wilson's intellectual inheritance. Wilson was not sent
into combat, so his reaction was less to bloodshed
than to the democratizing experience of being thrust
into relations with men of different backgrounds and
social classes. After the war, he wrote, he realized that
"I could never go back to the habits and standards of

even the most cultivated elements of the world in which I had lived. It now appeared to me too narrowly limited by its governing principles and prejudices. My experience of the army," he concludes, "had had on me a liberating effect."

Wilson was thus prepared for the next great immediate experience of his career, the writing he would help canonize in *Axel's Castle*. The New York intellectuals and the Southern intellectuals who eventually became known as the New Critics are associated with this same literature, but their exposure to it was almost entirely academic and after the fact. Wilson was already working as a critic when the major modernist works appeared; he was in many cases the first and the most authoritative reviewer in the field. He reviewed *The Waste Land* in the *Dial*; he reviewed *Ulysses* in the *New Republic*; he edited T. S. Eliot at *Vanity Fair*. F. Scott Fitzgerald, whose talent he mentored, was his college friend. He maintained a sense of personal involvement with the modernist movement, and this prevented his relation to that movement from ever becoming academic.

Wilson was, in short, a representative figure of what Richard Hofstadter later identified as the first generation of intellectuals in America. Wilson defined himself in reaction to what Hofstadter called "mugwump" culture—the culture of gentility, Anglophilia, and social conservatism. His enemies in his early years were the twentieth-century avatars of mugwumpery, Irving Babbitt, Paul Elmer More, and the rest of the New Humanists, writers Wilson accused of "preaching restraint

to a people already bound hand and foot." And he defined himself in relation to one of the institutions that
emerged in the beginning of the century to give these
new intellectuals a social and economic base—the institution of smart commercial journalism. Another institution that served as a base for intellectuals emerged at
the same time, the university humanities department.
But Wilson's relations with this institution were very
different, in ways that were, as it turned out, pivotal to
his writing and his cultural status.

After *Axel's Castle* Wilson turned to the history of
socialism, the project that produced *To the Finland
Station*, published in 1940. Socialism was a matter of
immediate and personal importance to most of the New
York intellectuals, but Wilson's relation to the subject
was different from theirs because he had had, so to
speak, a political identity before communism; and this
made it easier for him to have a political identity after
communism which was not defined entirely by its opposition to communism. In the case of many of the
New York intellectuals there is the sense that the rest
of their lives reduced to a matter of making up for the
great error of their credulousness about the Soviet experiment. With Wilson one never has this feeling. He
was quite clear, in *To the Finland Station*, about his
lack of enthusiasm for Marxist theory—something one
feels sprang from his lack of enthusiasm for Marx, as his
enthusiasm for Lenin sprang from an admiration of
what he regarded as the lonely and heroic quality of
Lenin's personality. When Wilson published the 1972
edition of the book, he criticized somewhat his own

portrait of Lenin. But he never transformed his disaffection with Leninism or the Soviet Union into a new kind of politics. This is why he was able to become an anti-Communist and yet oppose without reservation the cold war defense spending and the American involvement in Vietnam. Nor did his dislike of communism underwrite an approval of postwar Americanism—quite the contrary.

But the original publication of *To the Finland Station* marked a break in Wilson's career, and this break is what tends to be missed by the people who wonder where the Wilsons of today are. For, after 1940, Wilson no longer conceived of himself as a writer who was part of the social and cultural current he commented on. He instead conceived of himself as a writer who had stepped very deliberately out of the current. This revised self-conception was deliberate. Here is Wilson's own account of it, from an essay written in 1943: "There has come a sort of break in the literary movement that was beginning to feel its first strength in the years 1912–16, at the time I was in college at Princeton: the movement on which I grew up and with which I afterwards worked." This break in the literary movement was exacerbated, he goes on to say, by the failure of Marxism as a faith for writers and by the rise of what he called "the two great enemies of literary talent in our time: Hollywood and Henry Luce." Marxism, with no social field in which to play by the early '40s, moved to the English department, even as the English department usurped the cultural position of what Wilson called "the general man of letters."

In a passage from this midcareer essay, "Thoughts on Being Bibliographed," Wilson himself understands why there are no more Edmund Wilsons:

It is rather difficult for the veteran of letters of the earlier crop [his own generation] . . . to find an appropriate younger master on whom to bestow the accolade. On their side, the younger people want precisely to thrust him into a throne and have him available as an object of veneration. The literary worker of the twenties who had recently thought of himself as merely—to change the figure—attempting to keep alive a small fire while the cold night was closing down, is surprised and even further disquieted to find himself surrounded by animals, attracted or amazed by the light, some of which want to get into the warmth but others of which are afraid of him and would feel safer if they could eat him. What is wonderful to both these groups is that the man should have fire at all. What is strange is that he should seem to belong to a kind of professional group, now becoming extinct and a legend, in which the practice of letters was a common craft and the belief in its value a common motivation. The journalist of the later era is troubled at the thought of a writer who works up his own notions and signs his own name; and for the literary man in a college, incorporated in that quite different organism, the academic profession, with its quite other hierarchies of value and competitions for status, the literary man of the twenties presents himself as the distant inhabitant of another intellectual world; and he figures as the final installment of the body of material to be studied.

This convoluted passage starts with a throne and ends with a campfire. It's impossible to know what the metaphor is. I take this confusion in a writer famous for his lack of confusion to be a sign of genuine confusion in his thinking. For what the passage suggests rather clearly is that Wilson, by 1943, felt that the time in which intellectuals could imagine themselves engaged in the living work of the culture was over. For the journalist, he thought, there were only the twin seductions of Hollywood and Luce; for the professor, there was only the shadow world of scholarship and theory. The terms of the analysis should sound very familiar because they are exactly the terms one hears today from the people who wonder where the Wilsons have gone. Wilson himself was wondering the same thing.

Wilson's distaste for academic literary criticism was the pill in the mix of this revised assessment of his own cultural standing. Though he was friendly with some of its members, in particular with Allen Tate, he had little interest in the New Criticism, though it was, of course, the emerging academic critical school of his time. One reason for this disaffection was that the New Critics treated in an academic manner writing with which Wilson had felt personally engaged at the time it was being written. Books which he had known in their living state were now reduced to artifacts.

In 1943 Wilson was asked to write an essay on symbolist poetry for the *Kenyon Review*. "It is difficult for me to think of anything I should be less likely to write than an essay on the influence of Symbolist poetry," he complained in a letter to Tate. "I will go even further and say that it seems to me absurd in the extreme for the *Kenyon Review* at this time of day to devote a special number to the subject. And I will even go on to explain that I would not write anything whatever at the request of the *Kenyon Review*. The dullness and sterility and pretentiousness of the *Kenyon*, under the editorship of Ransom, has really been a literary crime." And he went on, in case the point had been missed: "Mary and I have both sent Ransom some of the best things we have written of recent years, and he has declined to print any of them. . . . Of Mary's book he published a stupid and impudent review apparently composed by the office boy; my books he has not reviewed at all."

In another letter to Tate, also from 1943: "I brought the Henry James number of the *Kenyon Review* back from New York and Mary has just read it all. I could only read it in patches, and she confirms my impression that it almost all sounds as if it had been written by the same person. . . . The Yeats number of the *Southern Review* was a monstrosity. It doesn't so much honor Yeats as make a fool of the *Southern Review* by the discrepancy suggested between Yeats and his commentators." And to his friend Helen Muchnic, also in 1943: "I am strongly reacting against academic communities after trying to do something with teaching and rather enjoying it at first. Now I've decided that the whole thing, for a writer, is unnatural, embarrassing, disgusting. . . . (Please don't tell them this, though, at Smith!)"

It's clear how elemental this disaffection was. Wilson was a critic who made a living from his writing—the New Critics were paid by universities. Their writing did not have to meet a commercial test, and they could therefore be as pretentious or pedantic as they liked, since pretension and pedantry were (from the journalist's point of view) what their structure of merit in fact rewarded. But it's also clear that Wilson wanted—why should he not have?—to be a part of their consideration of modern literature, and that he felt personally rebuffed by them. He responded, after 1943, by completely ignoring academic literary criticism. He never reviewed a single work by the New Critics—nothing by Brooks, Blackmur, Empson, or Richards. He ignored as well the work of F. O. Matthiessen and Kenneth Burke. He reviewed Trilling's first book, on Matthew Arnold, which he admired, but nothing by Trilling after that, not even *The Liberal Imagination*. He said that he never read Leavis's books because they were too dogmatic (a case of the preacher telling the salesman to shut up). He objected to Leavis for calling Max Beerbohm trivial. For his part, Wilson claimed, he had never bothered to read *Middlemarch*.

The whole history of animosity culminated in the famous essay "The Fruits of the MLA" (1968), probably the first text in the now-familiar genre of MLA bashing. "The Fruits of the MLA" is one of Wilson's finer moments, but it must be said that, among its other accomplishments, it raises peevishness to an art form. He noted with asperity, for instance, that the people at In-

diana University insist that their institution be called
Indiana University, and not the University of Indiana:
"Why can it not be referred to in the same way as any
other state university?" he barked. The New Critics
and the textual scholars Wilson was berating in "The
Fruits of the MLA" are not the people who are blamed
today for the eclipse of the style of criticism Wilson
represented. New Critics and textual scholars are the
heroes of the anti-English department reaction. But
they were not heroes to Wilson.

Wilson also—and this, too, seems underappreciated
by the sort of person who asks where the Wilsons of
today are—gradually lost his interest in canonical literature almost altogether. After *The Wound and the Bow*
and *The Triple Thinkers*, his critical attention became
absorbed by minor writers and minority cultures—
Haiti, Canada, the Essenes, the Iroquois. His refusal to
champion canonical figures had a perverse deliberate-
ness to it—so that in his enormous volume on the literature of the Civil War, *Patriotic Gore*, he devoted
many pages to James De Forest and Ambrose Bierce
but had almost nothing to say about Melville and Whitman. Wilson believed, in fact, that literature ought to
be thought about not canonically but comparatively,
and in an international context. He was, in the latter
half of his career, a sort of cultural globalist: he announced his desire to be thought of in that way in the
first essay in *The Bit Between My Teeth*, written in
1952. The notion that Wilson was a celebrant of the
Great Books is entirely mistaken.

So is the notion that Wilson was a champion of the
American Way. In 1952 the editors of *Partisan Review*

ran their now famous symposium on the supposed turn of American intellectuals toward American values—the symposium entitled "Our Country and Our Culture." It is a little ironic that the writer the editors cited in their introductory statement as signaling this new enthusiasm was Edmund Wilson: they quoted a passage about American cultural supremacy from *Europe Without Baedeker*, Wilson's report on postwar Europe, which had appeared in 1947. But Wilson himself does not appear in the symposium, and it is a good thing, for by 1952 he would have been the last intellectual in America to have rallied to the idea that American culture had suddenly become adequate to the life of the mind. Wilson despised postwar American society; his withdrawal to Wellfleet, on Cape Cod, and Talcottville, in upstate New York, was a carefully cultivated effort at detachment. The journals of his later years, beginning with *The Fifties*, are crowded with the ghosts of the deceased members of his literary generation—Fitzgerald, John Peale Bishop, Edna Millay, and so on. He discovered the advantages of the dinosaur persona, bohemian type, and he cultivated it for twenty years.

But there is a wrinkle in this story of the second half of Wilson's career, and that is that at the same time he was turning away from public life, he was being rediscovered by a new generation of readers, thanks to Jason Epstein's paperback reprints of Wilson's earlier books. The Anchor edition of *To the Finland Station* was published in 1952. It was followed by a collection from *The Triple Thinkers* and *The Wound and the Bow* entitled *Eight Essays*, then by an anthology of reviews from 1920 to 1950 called *A Literary Chronicle*, and then by the reprinting of Wilson's social reportage of the '20s and '30s in *The American Earthquake*. Wilson himself collected his shorter pieces in *The Shores of Light* (1950) and *Classics and Commercials* (1952), published by Farrar, Straus. The self-conscious withdrawal of the personal Wilson was accompanied by a massive cultural dose of the textual Wilson.

This had the effect of transplanting Wilson from what he regarded as his own generation of public intellectuals (that of Van Wyck Brooks and H. L. Mencken) to the generation of '50s and '60s intellectuals (that of Trilling and McCarthy and Howe). This second life gave Wilson much more intellectual freedom than he had enjoyed in his first life, since it allowed him to write on only what he chose. His stature had been established. He thus could abandon the role of champion—champion of modernism, or of socialist thought, or of Americanism—and express his reactions as it suited him. He could say, in *A Piece of My Mind* (an appropriately Wilsonian title), that "as an American, I have not the least doubt that I have derived a good deal more benefit of the civilizing as well as the inspirational kind from the admirable American bathroom than I have from the cathedrals of Europe." And then he could say, in *The Cold War and the Income Tax*, "I have come finally to feel that this country, whether or not I continue to live in it, is no longer any place for me." A few years later, he could turn around and propose the publishing venture that eventually became the Library of America. It would be nice if people who piously intone Wilson's name seemed as willing to countenance ambivalence as he was to practice it.

The public intellectual is not a universal type. This is not only because intellectuals change, but because publics change. One of the things we admire about Wilson is that he was faithful to the literature and ideas that mattered to him when he was young, and that he could see the value of becoming, in effect, a private intellectual when the culture no longer engaged his strongest sympathies. That this turn toward private interests did not make him any less a public figure is not a bad lesson for intellectuals who want to go public today.

WILSON AND OUR
NON-WILSONIAN AGE

PAUL BERMAN

Has the American culture that could once generate an Edmund Wilson become incapable of generating anyone similar today? Has a fundamental habit of mind changed in American life, and is the age of critics-in-general (and readers-in-general) behind us?

The idea that some such downward development has taken place was proposed by Russell Jacoby in *Dissent* in 1983, then was elaborated by James Atlas in the *New York Times Magazine* and again by Jacoby in a slightly muddled book called *The Last Intellectuals*. And from those long-ago seeds have subsequently blossomed ten thousand articles by as many authors, new articles all the time, embellishing the never-ending theme of a break or rupture in American intellectual life. *Then* we had thinkers and critics of independence and stature, the nonacademic essayists; *now* we have none, or almost none. The expositions of this idea have taken many strange turns. Yet the reality of a cultural shift is hard to dispute—and the nature of that reality and

some of its causes can be seen, I think, with a glance at
Wilson and his generation, born around 1895, and at
the generation of Atlas and Jacoby, writers of my own
age, born fifty or sixty years later.

These two generations have this in common: they
each underwent, in their youth, the disillusioning experience of watching America march off to a pointless
and devastating war—against Kaiser Germany or
against Communist Vietnam. And the response of a
certain number of very clever people from both generations was noticeably parallel, given a half century of
cultural evolution. The response was to turn with revulsion away from the ordinary sensibilities and sen-
timentalities of middle-class American life in favor of a
European avant-garde and radical leftism, always with
the hope of giving the radical ideas a new, American
twist. In Wilson's case, you can see in his diaries from
the 1910s and '20s and other early writings how passionately he felt those impulses. He served in France
during the Great War. Like Hemingway and Dos Passos, he worked in the medical corps. And when he got
back home he was not the same man as before. He
moved to Greenwich Village and took up a literary life
working for the magazines, feeling that he was doing
something very rebellious and radical. (Only in later
years did Wilson reinterpret this career of his as an ata-
vistic, conservative return to the archaic values of an
older American past.)

Rebelliousness led him to the French literary avant-
garde (and to a few of its English-speaking disciples)
and to the modernist devotion to the inner world of the
imagination. Then again he was attracted to the idea of

268 PAUL BERMAN

science, too, and to the study of the outer world. He
hoped that, from a union of literature and science, a
new avant-garde literature might emerge, something at
once romantic and neoclassical, modernist and naturalist—a literature that might point to a new way of living.
By the late '20s Wilson's dismay at American society,
his faith in science, and his more-than-literary hopes
for literature led him to Marxism, too. And each of
these stages in his career was recapitulated in a different form by a good number of the people who were
young a half century later.

The people who started out in the era of the Vietnam War—at least some of them—felt a noticeably
similar desire to withdraw from the American mainstream. The withdrawal led them to the (mostly)
French philosophical avant-garde and to the postmod-
ernist idea of uniting literature with science (in the
form of linguistics, whence semiotics and deconstruction). There was an idea of giving priority to the imaginary over the real—a great principle of the postmodern
style in philosophy and the arts. And there was the con-
tradictory idea of giving priority to the real over the
imaginary—therefore a turn to Marxism in a variety of
novel applications.

Yet, for all these parallels, the writing that resulted
was completely different. Wilson learned to write cultural journalism from the nineteenth-century French
critic Hippolyte Taine (who was, by the way, a main
founder of the idea of joining together science and literature). In Taine's eyes, therefore in Wilson's, cultural
journalism was an art—and the king of commentaries.
But what kind of literary aspiration took root among the

young intellectuals of a half century later? Instead of an ideal of cultural journalism there was an ideal of scientific-minded philosophy. Theory became king of commentaries. Instead of a devotion to serious literature there was a celebration of popular culture—partly in order to shock the older generation, partly out of a recognition that, by the '60s, the cultural categories of high and low had been scrambled by life and not by critics. And for a certain number of young people who felt those impulses, the right kind of career might be to take up guitar and join a rock band; or to dash off pop culture criticism in the anti-literary automatic-writing style of the countercultural weeklies; or, less daringly, to enter graduate school and become an avant-garde professor of cultural theory. But the right kind of career no longer had much to do with writing the kind of critical essay that Wilson might have admired.

Wilson and the writers who came along in the decades after him could feel that by devoting themselves to the art of the critical essay they were wrestling with the spirit of their own era. But the people who started out during the Vietnam War or in its aftermath, and who nonetheless took an interest in the kind of writing that Wilson produced, found themselves engaged in a slightly musty enterprise, drawn more to writers of an older generation than to writers of their own age. For no one could doubt that the real excitement of the moment lay in the enterprises that went under the name of theory, meaning Marxism, feminism, postcolonial studies, cultural studies, and so forth. And if you want to see the consequence of these developments, you have only to look at the ten thousand articles that, coming after the original presentations by Jacoby and Atlas, have pointed to a rupture in American intellectual life. The simple notion of an essayist in Wilson's style—of someone who writes artfully and knowledgeably for the literary-minded reader on broad topics—has faded so far into the past that, for any number of writers and editors today, the old idea has become nearly impossible to understand.

Jacoby introduced the term *public intellectual* to distinguish a writer like Wilson from the professors who address specialized, private audiences on narrow topics. But the term, having escaped from the lab, has mutated horribly until by now it has come to mean a professor—who, unlike other professors, has succeeded in getting on television or in being celebrated in magazine puff pieces. The term has come to express a fascination with the size of the audience (is someone's name recognized by millions?) or with political influence. But the question of what is actually written no longer seems to merit discussion. And so, the rupture is real enough, and ours is an age of the university department and the television set and the slick magazine, but it is not an age of the literary intellectual.

There may be one other similarity between Wilson's generation and the people who came of age during the Vietnam War. In the case of Wilson and his contemporaries, the original impulses that emerged from the Great War and the avant-garde of the '20s ran aground after a while, and everybody who had been caught up in the excitement of the years after the war had to change or go under. That moment occurred around 1940. A number of Wilson's friends died in that period, and a number of others—Dos Passos is an example—lost a part of their talent. Wilson himself went through some hard days. His old notion about an impending avant-garde breakthrough in literature was no longer sustainable. And his ideas about Marxism fell apart entirely.

These ideas of his, his Marxism, can be a little difficult for readers to make sense of today—which makes it hard to understand what the collapse of those ideas meant to him. Wilson's Marxism was his own concoction. In the early years of the Great Depression he was attracted to the Communist Party, but he turned against the Communists soon enough—warned against them by Dos Passos, who advised him (in a letter from May 1932) to "introduce a more native lingo" into his radicalism. And Wilson set out to do just that, philosophically as well as rhetorically. His idea was to mix together what he had learned from Taine with a few new concepts that had been developed by Max Eastman, the old editor of the *Masses*. From Taine, Wilson drew something of a positivist understanding of the advance of science and mankind. From Eastman (whom no one reads today, though he wrote wonderful things, with a wonderful lightness), he drew a pragmatist disdain for Marx's Hegelian reasoning, combined with an admiration for Lenin, the scientific-minded man of practical action (as Eastman imagined him to be).

Taine, Eastman, positivism, pragmatism—these influences put Wilson at odds with entire aspects of conventional Marxism. Reading him, you could almost conclude that he was arguing against Marxism itself. But not so. He wanted nothing to do with dialectical

philosophy or the legacy of Hegel, yet he was adamant
about historical progress, about the working class as the
bearer of that progress, about the notion of a scientific
understanding of society as the key to working-class action, and about the moral failure of capitalism. His
Marxism was peculiar, but it was Marxism.

Under its inspiration he produced his two books of
'30s social and political journalism, *The American Jitters* and *Travels in Two Democracies*. He wrote some
of the essays in *The Triple Thinkers* (the pieces on
Flaubert, John Jay Chapman, Shaw, and the not very
successful essay on Marxism itself) and in *The Wound
and the Bow* (especially the very moving essay on Dickens). He wrote *To the Finland Station*, which is not just
about Marxism but breathes its spirit—if you take
Marxism's spirit to be a dedication to human liberation
and not dogmatic fanaticism. Marxism, in short, animated a big portion of his best work, and the collapse
of his faith in it must have been a gloomy experience.

On the other hand, there's nothing like an intellectual collapse to stimulate new thoughts. The conventional opinion about Wilson's later work—the notion
that, after 1940, he scattered his energies on a variety
of marginal topics without a central theme—seems to
me not entirely accurate. If you read his later writings
in the light of his Marxism and its failure, it should be
obvious that, during the years from 1940 until his death
in 1972, he offered a series of replies to what he had
written previously: now arguing against the philosophical theories that had proven to be mistaken, now looking for alternatives to the Marxist future that had once
been his hope. The most ambitious of these later writ-

ings—his *Patriotic Gore*, about the literature of the
Civil War—ought to be read, it seems to me, as a re-
joinder to *Finland Station*. The whole point of *Finland
Station* was to show mankind's gradual achievement of
mastery over the laws of history—the rise of social
science, leading to political action to create a better
society, as undertaken by Lenin in the Bolshevik Revolution of 1917.

In developing this theme Wilson had the occasion to
quote Trotsky on the topic of the American Civil War
(from Trotsky's diatribe against liberals, *Their Morals
and Ours*). "History has different yardsticks for the cruelty of the Northerners and the cruelty of the Southerners in the Civil War," Trotsky said. "A slave-owner
who through cunning and violence shackles a slave in
chains, and a slave who through cunning and violence
breaks the chains—let not the contemptible eunuchs
tell us that they are equals before a court of morality!"
Already in writing *Finland Station* Wilson was uncomfortable with that kind of reasoning. But the purpose of
Patriotic Gore was to turn against it entirely. The book
on the Civil War really did hold the North and the
South as equals in the court of morality. Wilson saw
Lincoln as a species of tyrant, Bismarck-style, and for
the slaves he summoned no great sympathy.

These attitudes scandalized Wilson's liberal friends
at the time, and they scandalize us today, and the
temptation is strong to dismiss *Patriotic Gore*'s more
obnoxious passages as simple mischief-making. Wilson
did like to toy with his readers. But his intention, entirely serious, in making those remarks in *Patriotic
Gore* was to propose a countertheory to the idea of his-

tory that he had presented in *Finland Station*. He
wanted to argue that notions of progress—of world history advancing toward a scientifically determined superior endpoint—were merely a cover for the crimes
committed by people like Lenin and Trotsky. He
wanted us to fear power, instead of seeking to harness
it to projects that we think of as worthy.

Wilson never lost his young man's indignation
against the shape of modern society and market economics. But instead of looking for social alternatives in
a Marxist future he now began to look in back corners
of the society that already existed, in remote minority
cultures that had preserved some integrity of their own
against the depredations of mass culture and the capitalist economy. Or he looked into the distant past. The
social and political journalism that he wrote in the
1930s constituted his search for the socialist future, but
the journalism that he wrote after 1940—about ancient
Hebrews, modern Zuñis, Iroquois, French Canadians,
Haitians, and the gentry of upstate New York—constituted a search for a living past. The journalism of the
1930s corresponded to his Marxist idea of history, and
the journalism from the years after 1940 corresponded
to his anti-Marxist idea. The later work was a criticism
of the earlier, and was all the livelier for being so.

This turn in Wilson's writing offers a last resemblance to the generation that came along half a century
after his. We, too, seem to be going through a two-stage
development. The first stage—the radicalism of theoretical system building, with its anti-literary results—
lasted quite a few years after the Vietnam era, and in
some corners of the university will doubtless endure

into the distant future. Still, the generation that came up during the Vietnam era has sooner or later had to discover that "theory" and the various *isms* may have certain virtues, and may continue to display those virtues in the future—but theory and the isms cannot go beyond the limits of the academy, in some respects cannot even achieve the limits of the academy. When was that discovery made? Our equivalent of Wilson's 1940—when did it take place? I think that, for a good number of people, the discovery arrived in the mid-'80s, and it came in the form of the argument about a rupture in American intellectual life. For what did it mean to draw a distinction between *then*, the age of independent public intellectuals, and *now*, the age of the jargon-spouting professors? To my mind, drawing that distinction offered a way to express a weary frustration with the system-building theories. And it offered a way to counter them—not by constructing a new supertheory to replace the older ones, or by reverting to the pre-radical habits of the academy, or by taking up the dogmatism of the neoconservative table thumpers. The idea, instead, was to look over our shoulders, backward, to the age of *then*: to recognize the virtue of certain work from the past and of writers older than ourselves; to stop scorning the intellectuals from earlier generations; to take the best of them as models and to hold ourselves to their standards. Anyway, to give it a try. The idea was to heal the rupture in American intellectual life by the act of recognizing it.

AFTERWORD

SEAN WILENTZ

THE CENTENARY of Edmund Wilson's birth, first celebrated at the Mercantile Library in Manhattan, offered
Princeton's American Studies Program an opportunity
to pay belated homage to Wilson's memory. Like most
universities, Princeton has done a much better job in
honoring its financial benefactors, its statesmen and
politicians, and (now and again) its illustrious professors than it has in honoring its writers. The tire mag-
nate Harvey Firestone, who provided the necessary
funds for constructing the university's main library,
naturally had the building named after him. Adlai
Stevenson is remembered with Stevenson Hall; inside
Firestone Library there is a sublibrary called the John
Foster Dulles Library of Diplomatic History; and at
Forbes College (named for Malcolm's son, Steve),
there is even a little Norman Thomas Library. Christian Gauss, Wilson's great teacher and surrogate
father, is memorialized in the title of Princeton's pres-
tigious humanities seminar series. But of Wilson—as of
F. Scott Fitzgerald (who, admittedly, never graduated),
or John Peale Bishop, or any other Princeton novelist,

essayist, or poet going back to Hugh Henry Bracken-
ridge and Philip Freneau, class of 1771—the university
has taken little or no official notice.

To be sure, Wilson the critic did not exactly fit the
stereotype of the grateful and affable Princeton graduate. He dearly loved the place for its languid amenities
and certain inspiring instructors, as well as for undergraduate friends like Fitzgerald and Bishop. As a student, caught up in the idealism left over from Woodrow
Wilson's time as Princeton's president, he imagined
that the university was on the verge of becoming a re-
formed seat of great learning. Although the war and
then the '20s squelched that idealism, Wilson returned
to Princeton often over the years following his com-
mencement in 1916, mainly to visit Gauss, to whom he
dedicated *Axel's Castle*. In 1952, he offered a series of
Gauss Seminars rehearsing chapters for *Patriotic Gore*,
which he published ten years later; while in residence,
he treated his friend Leon Edel to running commentaries on the Princeton of forty years earlier.

But, apart from taking maximum advantage of the
bar and the sleeping quarters at the Princeton Club of
New York, Wilson displayed little interest in fostering
any wider or more formal alumni connections. He
was interested least of all in the extravagant, ritualized
nostalgia and financial largesse for which Princeton
graduates are famous. Wilson never had any money at
all, and the papers in his slender alumnus dossier, still
on file in the university's archives, chiefly document
his efforts to fend off, with considerable annoyance, his
alma mater's annual requests for a contribution. Some
of Wilson's classmates regarded him, in turn, not only

as a sometime Red (and, after *Hecate County*, as a pornographer), but, worse, as disloyal. A distinguished current member of the Princeton faculty tells of returning home for Christmas as a college freshman, circa 1950, excited at having just discovered Edmund Wilson's writings and eager to quiz his father, who had graduated in the great man's Princeton class.

"You mean *Bunny* Wilson?" the father snapped. "Sure, I remember Bunny Wilson. Never comes to reunions!"

Many of us who came of age in the universities of the '60s and early '70s first encountered Wilson as a forbidding public figure, the arbiter of literary excellence—austere, peremptory, and owlish, like David Levine's cartoons of him in the *New York Review of Books*. Whereas his classmates might have thought of him as a walking scandal, and generations of writers took him as a literary guide and man of letters, we saw him as a lordly and quarrelsome old man—an authority at a time when authorities were unfashionable. It was only thanks to the burgeoning paperback market that some of us discovered a Wilson more to our liking—the would-be historians and political radicals in *To the Finland Station* and *The American Earthquake*, artsier types in *Axel's Castle* and *The Wound and the Bow*. Each of us in his own way (Wilson, as I remember, mainly attracted male readers) could imagine the younger Wilson as a spiritual forerunner—a dissenter at odds with America's imperial complacency, a candid chronicler who wrote unashamedly (if a bit clinically) about his sex life, a critic as attuned to the pratfalls of

Charlie Chaplin as he was to the arabesques of high modernist fiction.

What we did not know at the time was that many of our elders had also encountered one Edmund Wilson, only to discover others. The left-wing writer Josephine Herbst, for example, recorded her astonishment at reading *I Thought of Daisy* in the '30s, after a brief meeting with Wilson at his apartment. "I had been deceived by the plump but graceful figure, the scholar's high brow, and the face, delicately larded with baby fat that might never wear off," Herbst recalled a quarter century later. "I had imagined the squire, the don, or oddly enough, even the choirboy, but not the amorous, complex nature he was attempting to unveil."

The commemorative proceedings at Princeton, which with those in Manhattan led to the present volume, had similar difficulty in pinning Wilson down. The plan was to assemble various writers and editors whose paths had crossed Wilson's, along with a younger cohort of reviewers, essayists, and editors whose work has been making its way in some of Wilson's old magazines, notably the *New Republic*, the *New Yorker*, and the *New York Review*. Apart from challenging the claim that the nonacademic intelligentsia is dead, the conference was meant to start a public conversation, across generational lines, about an exemplary figure—exemplary, as Ann Hulbert explained, not as a flawless thinker but as an outstanding writer of a certain kind of learned but accessible literary and cultural criticism.

We wound up with some unresolved paradoxes. Wilson, Jason Epstein explained, was essentially a man of the Enlightenment, who valiantly stuck by a faith in the powers of human reason despite the abundant modern evidence of reason's shortcomings. Yet he was also, as Barbara Epstein noted, a man of deeply romantic, almost Faustian intellectual ambitions and passions. At one point in the discussion, Arthur Schlesinger, Jr., claimed that Wilson "wasn't really a man of politics," and that he "ignored the New Deal, didn't always vote, focused on literature and personality and society." Yet at another point, Schlesinger observed that Wilson voted for Norman Thomas for "most of his life," was a "strong supporter" of John Kennedy and Robert Kennedy, and wore a McGovern-for-President button in 1972 (although, according to Jason Epstein, he may have worn the button to please his wife Elena, "who was an avid member of the League of Women Voters and took voting extremely seriously"). Throughout the conference, people puzzled over Wilson as an antimodern modernist—an early champion of literary modernism who, in his alienated later years, found pleasure and solace chiefly in the American past and in minority cultures that had resisted and somehow survived modernity's assaults.

One scholar who attended the conference observed that the more that any speaker knew about a particular theme or subject, the more likely he or she was to criticize Wilson's handling of it, while praising the power of Wilson's mind and the rest of his output. This was at any rate true of some of the younger critics. David Remnick did not budge from his critique of *To the Finland Station*'s mandarin leftism, and of Wilson's naive original portrait of the "selfless" Lenin as a dictator despite himself. Randall Kennedy and David Bradley, speaking in very different tones of voice, would not let Wilson off the hook for ignoring, they said, important black writers. Whereas C. Vann Woodward, the dean of modern American historians, remarked that Wilson's *Patriotic Gore* is tougher on Yankee myths than it is on their Confederate equivalents, Paul Berman and Andrew Delbanco went further, suggesting, as Delbanco put it, that the South is really the book's hero "because it is the region that stands against the monster"— namely, the despotic centralized state. Jed Perl highly praised Wilson's eye, while Wendy Lesser faulted his ear and what she called Wilson's tendency "to turn what others would take largely as sound experiences into visual or intellectual experiences." In sum, for all of his brilliance as a journalist and critic, Wilson misjudged the moral crisis over black slavery and the moral crisis over Bolshevism—certainly among the greatest moral crises that the Republic has endured over the last two hundred years. And he was weak on modern American poetry.

Yet no one at the conference, young or old, was willing to leave things at that. For even in what some consider his crankier moments, Wilson offered important counterpoints and correctives to his own major themes. Thus, in *To the Finland Station*, there are premonitions, as Michael Walzer and others indicated, of the coming Marxist disaster—including a powerful analysis of what Wilson called "the sadistic element" in Marx's writings. Thus, in *Patriotic Gore*, the notorious sections mocking the combatants' moral pretensions (especially the North's) sit alongside Wilson's startling apprecia-

tion of the greatness of Ulysses S. Grant's memoirs—
not to mention the writings of Abraham Lincoln and
Mary Chesnut. Delbanco describes the book as a classic in its account of "the simultaneous human aspiration for transcendence and the descent into violence
and vengeance." David Bromwich calls Wilson "a heroic historian of the resistance to fashion" by the modern artist. Wherever Wilson was engaged in elucidat-
ing a literary style, his genius as a reader and explainer
did not flag. And here, at least to this American historian, is one of the lasting marks of Wilson's power.

It has been said of the New York intellectuals who
arrived on the scene just after Wilson that they suffered from overdoing two tendencies—a tendency to
interpret literature in political terms and a tendency to
interpret politics in literary terms. The first was a natural effect of '30s Marxism and its fallout; the second,
however, owed a great deal directly to Wilson's example. But if, as with Wilson's assessment of Lenin, the
literary approach to politics and history has shown
some glaring weaknesses, it has also shown enormous
strengths, illuminating social and psychological features of the past that went unnoticed by conventional
American historians and biographers—for example, his
poignant portrait of the avenging brute, William Te-
cumseh Sherman, who died rereading *Great Expecta-
tions,* and of Sherman's strange son Tom. Historians
today are supposed to have taken a linguistic turn, and
launched into the story of how half-known discursive
structures have shaped the world. Wilson, the old his-
toricist who combined eighteenth-century rationalism
and nineteenth-century materialism, would have been

dubious. But by expanding his literary critic's art to cover past politics as well as literature and philosophy, he helped enlarge the scope of American historical understanding—and, not incidentally, helped a younger generation of talented and still-influential writers and scholars (including Alfred Kazin and Richard Hofstadter) find its voice.

What these contributions, among others, portend for Wilson's future standing among American authors is still unclear. Some other writer-critic—one thinks immediately of Robert Penn Warren, ten years Wilson's junior—may rival him as the nation's greatest contribution to twentieth-century letters. (Warren surpassed Wilson as a poet and novelist, though Wilson's was the better expository style, and, of course, his the greater range.) Much depends on what becomes of the smart commercial literary journalism in which Wilson excelled—a matter which the Princeton conference debated inconclusively. (Its current vigor certainly has something to do with the interest in Wilson's writing.) Finally, Wilson's criticism and history must be played off against the enduring value of his journals, which may well survive alongside *The Education of Henry Adams*.

The Princeton conference ended, as this volume ends, more encouraging than not. Wilson remains as elusive and as fascinating as ever, not because he was at all obscure but because there are so many different Wilsons to appreciate, sometimes in a single piece of his work. Although some polemicists tried to enlist him posthumously as an archconservative in the recent culture wars, he was anything but a celebrant of America's fables or of the idea of a literary canon. (Indeed, one might even read some of the attention paid to multiculturalism and to neglected American writers of quality as an extension of Wilson's literary predilections, though the connection may be accidental.) On the other hand, he was at heart an old-fashioned humanist, who aimed—as he wrote of the great modernists in the last sentence of *Axel's Castle*—to "break down the walls of the present" and wake us to "the untried, unsuspected possibilities of human thought and art."

INDEX

NOTE: Works cited are by Wilson unless otherwise identified

Library of Congress Cataloging-in-Publication Data

Edmund Wilson : centennial reflections / Lewis M. Dabney, editor.
p.   cm.
Papers originally presented at two symposia held at the Mercantile
Library of New York and at Princeton University in 1995.
Includes index.
ISBN 0-691-01672-0 (cloth : alk. paper).
ISBN 0-691-01671-2 (pbk. : alk. paper)
1. Wilson, Edmund, 1895–1972—Knowledge—Literature—
Congresses.   2. American literature—History and criticism—
Theory, etc.—Congresses.   3. Historiography—United
States—History—20th century—Congresses.   4. Criticism—
United States—History—20th century—Congresses.
5. United States—Intellectual life—20th century—
Congresses.   I. Dabney, Lewis M.
PS3545.I6245Z614   1997
818'.5209—dc21   97-12888